THE POWER OF
THINKING
DIFFERENTLY

An Imaginative Guide To
Creativity, Change,
& the Discovery Of New Ideas

This book is published by Hyena Press
2310 Homestead Rd, C1 #125
Los Altos, CA 94024
www.HyenaPress.com

Printed and bound in the United States of America.

Although the author and publisher have made every effort to ensure the accuracy and completeness of information contained in this book, we assume no responsibility for errors, inaccuracies, omissions, or any inconsistency herein. Any slights on people, places, or organizations are unintentional.

First Paperback Edition

ISBN 0984223932

Cover art: Christine Nolasco
Book design: Susan Reed
Editing: Liza Joseph

ATTENTION CORPORATIONS, UNIVERSITIES, COLLEGES, PROFESIONAL ORGANIZATIONS—DISCOUNT ON BULK PURCHASES AVAILABLE.

For information, please contact the publisher:
www.HyenaPress.com, info@hyenapress.com, (408) 329-4597

This book is dedicated to all those
who have inspired me:

To all of my friends who have dared
to try something new and who have
shown the courage to be different.

To the child I once was and every
adult I see who plays with ideas in a
childlike spirit.

Contents

participated in comedy improvisation. However, I could never marry what I was being taught in a corporate seminar with what I was doing as a creative human being outside of the corporate world. That was unfortunate because, looking back on it now, a lot of the material was quite useful. It just needed to have been taught in a more personal, meaningful context.

By looking at the brain and how human beings think, I hope to put common sense and *thinking differently* in a context that can help us generate new ideas, perspectives, and solutions to problems. For instance, by taking a look at neuroscience, psychology, popular creativity texts, and real life examples of creativity, this book explores why it can be hard to deviate from conventional wisdom. Through this exploration, you'll discover how you can break free of groupthink and creative blocks in order to arrive at creative insights.

This book also surveys many popular notions of the creative process from various perspectives (art, business, spirituality, science, amongst many others) and then spends the majority of the time laying out a single detailed map based on all these perspectives. The result is a map applicable to anyone or any group wanting to participate in the adventure of manifesting something new.

Many of us want to make a positive change in our lives, and in the effort, we often spend day after day banging our heads against a brick wall. Maybe, you are head of state and are trying to solve the Middle East crisis, the economic crisis, or global warming but are frustrated and upset that you have difficulty finding a successful solution.

On a wee bit smaller scale, maybe, you crave to use creativity in any number of ventures including…

- Changing careers
- Reorganizing your finances
- Starting a new business
- …a new painting
- Choreographing a dance routine
- Designing a new product or the next great invention
- Coming up with a new marketing plan
- Composing a new song
- Improving your relationships
- Concocting a new dish

- Solving a community problem (big)
- Stopping gang violence (huge)
- Discovering possible cures for diseases (huge)
- Authoring a book (enormous!)

…just to name a few, and you find yourself flooded with negative thoughts and energies because you have yet to find new ideas or are unable to successfully turn your great idea into a reality.

Or perhaps you desire a new path for your life, but are seemingly stuck in the mud, unable to play with it in order to see or realize alternatives.

Whatever your endeavor is, if you want to discover a new way to do whatever it is you're doing, this book presents a path to help you find your way. It is a book about how to get beyond the boundaries of common sensibilities in order to explore the world of creative possibilities.

How This Book is Organized

Part I

The first part of this book is the "what" section. It takes a look at our common thinking patterns and creative thinking from a bird's-eye view so we can see "what it all looks like."

Part II

The second part of this book is the "how" section. This is where we get down to the meat of the book. It addresses two important questions: How does the brain operate with respect to the different ways of thinking referenced in Part I, and how can we participate in the creative process? This section not only refers to the science of the way we think, but also describes the different stages of the creative process in an easily understandable way—through the language of a hero's journey.*

Part II is the map for the *Creative Journey* and is broken up into six

---

* The idea of describing the creative process as a hero's journey was inspired by Christopher Vogler's text for screenwriters entitled *The Writer's Journey.*

† Though I often refer to the stages of the creative process it may be more accurate to think of them as aspects, since the creative process is often non-linear. Writing the process in terms of stages simply makes for a more interesting narrative. Chapter 17 speaks more to this point.

CHAPTER ONE
Looking Beyond Our Island

Scenario 1: Imagine a man not unlike many other men. This particular man was born in 1980 and died in 2000. However, in 2000, he died at the age of 27. How is this possible?

A World of Creative Change

Too often we feel unable to change. We react to our circumstances with old, habitual responses—the ones that we use because we have always used them. And when we have the urge to respond differently, we have difficulty thinking of alternatives, like the writer who is confronted with writer's block—unable to conjure up the right line of dialogue, the right ending to their book, or just simply unable to write at all.

We all experience this type of creative block in various forms: unable to find a new way to deal with a dilemma, unable to manifest a unique idea, or unable to see alternative ways of living our lives. In essence, creative blocks just block us from accessing a different perspective, which is the same reason many will have trouble making sense out of the scenario above.

However, we are born creatures of transcendent ideas, new methods, ingenuity, inventiveness, and inspired works. Flying was thought to be only for birds until 1902 when the Wright brothers invented the propeller and stuck it on to a carefully designed glider. Copernicus drastically altered our worldview by conceptualizing a sun-centered astronomy at a time when the earth was the de-facto center of the universe. The paintings of Jackson Pollack, the poetry of Maya Angelou, and the plays of Neil Simon continue to enrich and inspire the lives of people today.

23

Who will ever forget Simon's famous commentary on art: "If no one ever took risks, Michelangelo would have painted the Sistine floor."*

Throughout human history, there have been numerous examples of extraordinary individuals who possessed revolutionary perceptions of themselves and society. Think of all those who have inspired social justice or have fought for equality. Mahatma Gandhi saw past his own meek appearance and past the apparently overpowering strength of the British Empire to recognize the power of non-violent, moral persuasion. By doing so, he not only led India to independence, but also had a positive effect on civil rights movements around the world.

There are also those individuals that are just seemingly able to experience fuller, more interesting lives than most—people who seemingly have a knack for finding alternatives and perceiving opportunities and are able to reframe their lives to better handle life's rough edges. There are those that are able to write their books, start their businesses, build real estate empires, and enjoy aspects of life that others struggle with.

What Do Creative People Have In Common?

It is true, many individuals and groups have the benefit of special circumstances and exemplary gifts. But some sort of inborn "specialness" is not the common factor for being creative. The power to think differently is not a product of a common IQ or environment. Nor is it a product of a common diet or exercise program. Creative people do not all eat special brain foods, drink ginkgo biloba enhanced smoothies, live on the street, or perform exotic one-thumbed push-ups.

According to Harvard psychiatry professor Albert Rothenberg, the only consistent characteristic for creativity is the motivation to be creative.[1]

The one common bond between all who think differently is their willingness to do so.

Without the desire to free India from British rule, Gandhi would not have made political change through non-violent protest. New works

---

* Nor is it easy to forget his famous quote on fear: "He's too nervous to kill himself. He wears his seat belt in a drive-in movie."

to get beyond our dominant modes of thought, our common sense, so that we can think differently. By having a lighthearted approach to life, we are able to shift perspectives in order to attain those aha moments of insight that are often the hallmark of the creative process.

However, a sense of humor isn't all we need. It is through cooperation between common sense and creative thought we are able to tackle problems that we haven't faced before, such as the man in the hospital. Otherwise, we'll be lost wandering around with tons of interesting ideas, but never being able to turn any of them into a tangible reality. We would be stuck chasing dreams, but never be able to manifest them in our waking lives. We would be able to access multiple interpretations of a setup, but never really able to get the humor out of a punch line.

Saved Through Stories

Although we can be limited by the stories we habitually tell ourselves, we can also be changed by finding new ones as they open up our view of the field of possibilities. By being able to see the world through the stories of others, we can better communicate with those that do not think like us. By expanding the number of stories we tell ourselves of how the world works, we not only have access to new ideas and solutions, but we can also deepen the meaning of our own lives.

Through others' and our stories, through old and new stories, we can think of our dilemmas and our experiences in news ways using imagery, symbolism, and anecdote, all of which help exercise both our faculties of reason and creativity. And, especially through humorous stories, we can attain shifts in our perspective that are both meaningful and memorable.

It is for these reasons that, throughout this book, I reframe my understanding of the creative process using the figurative language of mythology and through the tale of *The Island of Pickles and Doughnuts*.

Creativity for All

In many ways, the creative process is a means of increasing the degrees of freedom in our lives. The more conscious we are of the options and possibilities inherent in every decision, the less restricted we may feel—whether it is being more creative with our careers or finances, or whether it is discovering better ways to use our time. Though creative thinking can make our lives complex by providing us with the capability of doing more of what we desire, it can also simplify our lives by helping us be more efficient or by helping us perceive the extraordinary within the ordinary.

Many of our thinking habits are useful and are necessary for our survival. Yet there are always more ways to perceive and act in the world than through our habitual perceptions and behaviors. We can be hypnotized by the relative success of these habits—or the relative lack of pain from past failures—to wake up to this fact. We have the innate ability to do differently, yet too often we do the same, knocking our heads against the wall wondering why nothing has changed simply because time has passed.

But, in order to find new possibilities and explore all the alternatives the world has to offer, we must first believe that something different is even possible.

We must first believe that there is more to life than our island of pickles and doughnuts.

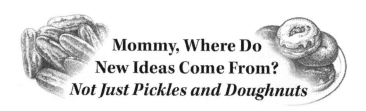

Mommy, Where Do New Ideas Come From?
Not Just Pickles and Doughnuts

One spring day, after the winds had died down, after cloudy night skies finally gave way to stars, when the moon was in the seventh house, and Jupiter was aligned with Mars, the most extraordinary thing occurred.

The carnival arrived.

It was the one day out of every pickle year that the people of the village took time out of their pickle and doughnut lives to do something different. But this was the first time in a long time that the carnival arrived right after a great storm.

The carnival occurred annually, and all the villagers attended annually. It was a festival full of sideshow freaks that included a sword swallower, a bearded lady, and an extraordinarily strong man. The villagers always marveled at the site, wondering what bad batch of doughnuts the bearded lady must have eaten, what finely made ones the strong man must have eaten, and where the swordsman ever found such an astonishingly long pickle.

Yet this wasn't all. The carnival was also well populated with various booths and stages of fast talking barkers—salesmen of all sorts with their rapid speech and flashy signs, who were trying to sell the latest miracle drug, potion, or device. The villagers were all very impressed by the problems these fantastic products could cure, fix, and improve. Even more than this, they were astounded by the stories the barkers told of how they came to discover and invent such amazing panaceas.

The fast moving lips and high-energy motions would also always excite the villagers, but the barkers spoke in a language that was too foreign and too quick for the villagers to truly understand what was being hocked to them. Every year a handful of villagers would become inspired enough to buy a barker's products. But without a strong understanding of the product, the miracle panacea would eventually find its way to an obscure corner of the villager's doughnut hut—forgotten after only a few days.

At the end of this particular carnival day, after the sun had begun to set and the carnival tents began to fall, a small group of fanciful villagers began to unknowingly assemble by the old oak tree that stood just outside the carnival grounds. There was the village chef, the village doughnut maker, the laborer, the farmer who employed the laborer, and a religious person. They all had their heads in the clouds, their minds spinning with possibilities that were inspired by the barkers. Their thoughts so preoccupied them that they did not notice one another. Nor did they notice the poor beggar that was unsuccessfully trying to fall asleep under the oak tree.

Their attention collapsed back into the present moment as the last of the villagers stumbled out from the carnival.

"I've got it!" cried the village drunk. "I've got it!"

"Me too!" replied the farmer, as his thoughts returned to earth.

"Me three!" replied the laborer.

The chef began to laugh. "I thought I was the only one who made sense out of what those barkers were saying."

"No. I was there too," added the religious person. "I was seeing the exact same things you were. I heard of all the wonderful stories of how they came to discover their strange new medicines and devices. But I thought I was the only one who put it together, who was inspired by the barkers' tales to come up with a way to generate new ideas—ones that can help us change the village."

"No. I put it together as well!" remarked the doughnut maker. "Let's fry up some new ideas."

They all then began looking at each other with large grins. None of them had left with any of the barkers' products, but from what they had experienced that day, they each had a sense of what it would take to create change. After listening to the barkers tell their tales of how they invented or discovered their panaceas, the villagers each believed they had found the keys to discovering new ideas and finding new ways of living their pickle and doughnut based lives.

"Then it is agreed," said the laborer. "In order to generate new ideas, we must work hard and then hope for some lucky accident which will drop a new idea upon our laps."

The others stared at him with bewilderment. "What?" the chef yelled out. "You're crazy! What we are supposed to do is immerse ourselves in an intersecting stream of ideas. Like adding ingredients to a soup, we are to gather as many different perspectives as possible, and see what new flavor arises."

"Were you two paying attention to anything that was going on in the carnival?" asked the doughnut maker. "We are to do the opposite of what you just recommended, chef. We are to take ourselves out of our familiar ideas. In order to find something new, we need to extract ourselves from our old soup of ideas, just like extracting a doughnut from old oil."

The farmer spoke up saying, "The opposite, yes, but not of the chef. We need to do the opposite of my employee, the laborer. In order to attain new insights, we need not lift a finger. Rather, we must have patience and wait for them to arrive. Just like waiting for pickles to grow before we harvest them."

The drunk took a sip from his flask and then lifted it up toward his companions. "It is much simpler than that my friends. This here is the magic potion …" he paused to unleash an odorous burp, "… that will help us come up with a new way of seeing things."

The religious person took hold of the flask. "That may have its effects, my friend. But it is nothing compared to the true source of creative ideas. The spirits within this bottle are miniscule compared to the creative spirits that are available to us from the divine."

Suddenly, the great buzz that pervaded the group of villagers at the outset of their encounter was reduced to mumbles. Their excitement plummeted to the earth as if overwhelmed by the island's gravity.

The beggar looked up from the ground and started giggling. Yet the villagers ignored him, too engrossed in their own puzzlements to have heard his chuckles.

"But how could this be," the laborer wondered shaking his head. "We were all together throughout the carnival…we saw the same things, we heard the same things. How could we have different perceptions of how to attain new ideas? Which one of us is right?"

CHAPTER TWO
Constellating the Creative Process

How do I find new ideas? Let me count the ways…

My local library and bookstore are well stocked with books that are in some way addressing creativity. Often during my research, I have found myself overwhelmed by the number of books and theories that describe the creative process. Maybe, you've felt the same way.

Oftentimes, advocates of creative thinking—or those that claim to have techniques to cultivate it—speak to one aspect of the term and completely neglect all others. For example, a book on creativity may address it within the context of business and fail to make any translations to the context of the artist or the parent. Conversely, another may associate creativity solely with the artist.

What follows is a magical mystery tour that visits several descriptions of the creative process. This whirlwind exploration is meant to give you a quick glimpse of the many ways people approach the creative process. Through a bird's eye view of what you are getting into, I hope to prepare you for *how* to think differently.

Visiting all perspectives is beyond the scope of our tour, for, as they say, there are many ways to skin a cow (or is it milk a cat?). Additionally, many of the perspectives we'll visit will not have clear fences separating them. The intention of this tour is simply to share with you a few of the prominent views held by several creative guides I have come across in my creative travels. Access to multiple perspectives opens up possibilities, and reflecting on the creative process itself is no exception.

Let us begin this tour by riding up to the top of the observation tower, and I will do my best to point out the highlights of the landscape.

The actual journey through the terrain will come in the chapters that follow.

The Magic of Creative Genius

From our view high above the creative landscape, a typical creative tourist will quickly point out how the creative process looks miraculous. They may see the piercing prose of Alice Walker, the improvisational outpouring of Robin Williams, or the scientific ingenuity of Einstein and stand in breathless awe at their works—completely convinced that creativity is only for a select few.

To the untrained eye, creativity can look like the result of some unexplainable magic—a mysterious undertaking reserved for the wizards, not accessible to us Muggles. However, on closer inspection, we find that many of these wizards have often experienced the same setbacks as the rest of us. For instance, Robin Williams was voted least likely to succeed by his classmates, and Einstein was labeled by one of his teachers as "mentally slow."

In fact, many creativity texts that talk about inventors and artistic geniuses seem to point to serendipity and perseverance as a common underlying factor of their creative process. In other words, within this context, creativity appears to be the result of hard work, skill, and in some sense, luck.

The Genius of Mozart

"People err who think my art comes easily to me. I assure you dear friend, nobody has devoted so much time and thought to composition as I."

Mozart is often thought of as an example of creative genius. Yet music did not flow unimpeded from his mind onto staff paper like water through a garden hose. He did not simply turn on his creative faucet at will. Mozart had to work hard to birth his material. His musical muscles received such a strenuous workout that, by the age of twenty-eight, Mozart had deformed hands because of all the hours he had spent practicing, performing, and composing.

Additionally, Mozart did not grow up in a musical vacuum. His father, Leopold Mozart, was also a gifted composer and expert violinist and spent a good deal of time teaching his son music theory. Mozart may have been gifted, but especially so in the sense that he was born to a father so well versed in music.

Realizing that behind Mozart's wizardry lay hours of practice, work, and musical experimentation can help make his creative process more familiar and accessible to us.

Pasteur and the Kellogg Brothers

Fanciful tales, such as Newton under the apple tree, Benjamin Franklin flying his kite during a storm, or Bill Gates' incident with elf-sized toilet paper (*ah...that's micro soft!*), often surround impactful inventions or discoveries.*

One of my favorite examples is Louis Pasteur's discovery of a vaccination for cholera. While performing experiments, he accidentally gave some chickens an old culture of the bacteria. He monitored and further tested these chickens, though he fully expected them to die from the old batch of cholera. Instead, what he found was that they had become immune, able to survive new cultures.

Though a lucky accident, it changed the initial perception that bacteria causing cholera always bring on the illness. This opened up the possibility of using inert bacteria as vaccination to develop immunity. It gives some credence to the idea that our initial perceptions may limit us from seeing the possibilities that lie beneath the surface.

The same is true of the Kellogg brothers, who accidentally ill prepared a batch of grain. At the time, grain was usually eaten warm, but because it had been ill prepared, the brothers had the idea of serving it cold instead. Though the idea, at first, seemed to be a silly attempt to utilize the mistake—and experts predicted failure, the brothers' "cornflakes" were a success and are still eaten today.

Though Pasteur and the Kellogg brothers were in some sense *lucky*, they all had to work hard prior to and after their run-in with chance. First, they needed to work hard prior to their serendipitous event to interpret it as a meaningful occurrence. The Kellogg brothers were primed by their knowledge of grain to eventually conceive of serving it cold. Without his many hours in the laboratory, Pasteur would not

---

* This is a joke. I do not know of any interaction between Mr. Gates and the elf community. Nor do I know if elf toilet paper is actually soft. It very well could feel like sandpaper.

have been able to explain why his cholera-exposed chickens became cholera resistant.

Furthermore, they all had to work hard after their creative insight in order to make their ideas a reality. The Kellogg brothers had to reproduce their ill prepared grain for public consumption, while Pasteur had to do more tests to verify he had truly discovered a cholera vaccination.

In some ways, it is very hard to look beyond the myth of creative genius. It can be hard to think that a Salvador Dali painting or an Emily Dickinson poem is the product of some sort of serendipity. But, according to this framework, hard work and perseverance can place us in a position to be more "lucky-accident" prone—better able to see opportunities where others might see only misfortunes.

Our creative tourists may object to this perspective by pointing to the fact that no matter how hard we work, there is no way we could be the next Da Vinci or the next Madame Curie. *There's no way I could have worked hard enough and have been lucky enough to have created the Mona Lisa or to have come up with the theory of radioactivity.* While this may be true, there weren't any Da Vincis before Da Vinci or Curies before Curie either (not counting their parents of course, but I'm sure you get my meaning).

The point isn't that you can necessarily replicate somebody else's creativity, but that you can enhance your own—that you can arrive at your own unique ideas.

You may not be the next Mozart, but you can definitely be a more creative you.

Stepping into Intersecting Streams: Generating Creative Ideas[1]

From the vantage point of the observation tower, another creative tourist observes that the creative process could also entail mixing a diversity of ideas and ingredients and observing what unique flavors arise. It may look like the unique combination of ideas of the Minotaur or the diverse array of ingredients found in a Chili Surprise.

For instance, you'll never know what you'll get by mixing leftover liver and pumpkin pie until you try. Or say, you are a painter looking for new inspiration for your next work, a science teacher looking for a new way to teach electromagnetism, a chef trying to improvise because you are ill equipped, or a businessperson searching for a new product. What kinds of ingenious ideas can you come up with if you only had a hammer to work with? What interesting devices can you imagine if you tried intersecting a hammer with these different needs?

Well, by entering the intersection of multiple perspectives a hammer could become a unique ink stamp, an electrical conductor, a garlic crusher, or a bookmark geared towards the do-it-yourself crowd.

Had you been crazy enough with your concoctions, you may have even been the first to stumble upon the iced coffee, the protein shake, or the corn dog.

Diversify Through Collaboration

The simplest way to enter such an intersection is by being immersed in a diverse group of people. Smith Miller, former CEO and Chairman of Royal Dutch/Shell, has found that unique concepts often arise through such interaction.

> You begin to find that you get some really neat ideas generated from creating a culture where people of different ethnicities, cultures, backgrounds, countries...come together.[2]

The writer, choreographer, musician, and problem solver often produce unique works and solutions through collaboration with others or by exposing themselves to other's works.

- The very unlikely pairing of David Bowie and Bing Crosby produced one of the most popular Christmas recordings of all time.
- Jazz musician and instructor Jamey Aebersold advocates listening to jazz recordings and live performances of other musicians in order to become a better jazz improviser.
- During World War II, the Allies initially had difficulty breaking the German coding system and were unable to decipher the communications transmitted between German submarines. At the time, cryptologists usually came from the field of linguistics. However, it took a British collaboration of mathematicians, scientists, classicists, chess grand masters, and crossword addicts to decipher the code.[3]

We often have preconceptions about what others can bring to the table. And we often have an adverse feeling towards those that have views different from our own. But the point is this: In order to get beyond our own limited perceptions, we need to allow ourselves to be immersed in different ones.

It may feel awkward, but the next time you are in need of some interesting ideas, you may want to invite over the most unlikely group of characters and just see what arises. Though their individual ideas may not be what you are looking for, they may provide you with novel inspiration for your own creative insights.

Diversifying Ourselves

In addition to collaborating with others, you can step into the intersection by becoming a diverse individual. One way to do this is through immersion into a new culture, whether it be ethnic, class, professional, organizational, or otherwise. The CEO may arrive at a new idea by spending some time in the shoes of their lowest level employees. The wealthy may arrive at new insights by living amongst the poor. Or creative associations may arise after experiencing life in another country. Howard Schultz arrived at his ideas for Starbucks after noticing the intimate relationship Italians had with coffee.

Simply putting yourself in a new environment other than your predominant one may expose you to new thoughts because you are surrounded by new stimuli. Step out of your normal confines and onto the sidewalks of your town. The color of the evening sky may inspire your next painting. The falling leaves of spring may inspire your next poem. And a stroll through your commercial streets may inspire your next business idea.

On my street, I see a postal store and a Mexican restaurant.

Oh! How about burritos delivered by mail? (It's just an idea.)

The most common means of diversifying yourself is through a type of direct research—groping for ideas until a few coalesce into something interesting. By continually learning new things, you can progressively grow a stable of concepts from which you can make new associations. An author may look to learning about the judicial system or read police reports in preparation for a crime novel. And a clothing designer may browse around a fabric store or walk through the mall for inspiration for their next design.

You can also expand your stable of concepts by simply following a diversity of interests. Frank Herbert, the author of the science fiction novel *Dune*, was a very diverse individual. His background included being a photographer, oyster diver, judo instructor, and jungle survival instructor, among many other things. This diversity of interests provided him with a wealth of ideas that he was able to interconnect in his science fiction epic. Gandhi, though of a Hindu background, studied the ideals of Christ, Buddha, the Baghavad Gita, and was inspired to manifest a nonviolent, mass political movement.

Like an expert chef, these individuals were able to turn their soup of ideas into something meaningful and unique. Though we may not all end up writing epic novels or leading political movements, we can all create our own distinctive stews. Just don't be discouraged if it initially causes your stomach to feel a bit queasy (especially if your burrito arrived through overnight delivery). From this perspective, the creative process calls for gathering as many interesting ideas as possible; the filtering and fine-tuning can always come later.

Stepping Out of the Stream: Non-Linear Problem Solving and Divergent Thinking

Many of the creative tourists on the observation tower find that, though they may immerse themselves in a diversity of ideas, it is often their own rigidity in thought and behavior that prevents them from truly entering the intersection. In other words, the accumulation of knowledge can help with creativity, but it is useless unless we are able to synthesize it in unique ways. For example, no matter how many areas of study we participate in, it is only by letting go of our dominant perceptions of a hammer that we can make new associations, such as realizing its potential as a garlic crusher, percussion instrument, or fly swatter—though I do not advocate the latter.

Fresh Eyes

It is in this spirit that creativity speaker Ernie Zelinski believes that being creative is the key to living in a changing world.

Creative people are flexible people.... What survives on earth is what effortlessly adapts to the changing environment and changing circumstances. Your flexibility will help you change plans in midstream, respond to the unexpected at a moment's notice, or rearrange a schedule without experiencing emotional turmoil.[4]

Perceiving the world with fresh eyes will make you more flexible and less bound by dominant ideas within a particular field. In his book *The Structure of Scientific Revolutions*, Thomas Kuhn notes, "Almost always the men who achieved…fundamental inventions of a new paradigm have been either very young or very new to the field whose paradigm they changed." For instance, it was an artist named Samuel Morse that invented the telegraph, while an accountant designed the Coca-Cola logo.

This just goes to show that expertise does not always lend itself to creativity, and that novice perspectives may be more insightful than we think.

Lateral Thinking

So, while a few creative tourists view the creative process as a *stepping into a stream* of intersecting ideas, a few others articulate the creative process as a *stepping out of a stream*. While the intersection model emphasizes entering into new connections of ideas, this stepping out model emphasizes exiting firmly ingrained beliefs, paradigms, and perceptions. As a result, it is often referred to as divergent, breakthrough, out-of-the-box, or lateral thinking.

The latter term was made famous by psychology professor Edward de Bono. *Lateral* is meant to contrast logical, straight ahead, brute force linear thought that he terms *vertical*. Imagine that problem you were barreling through or that creative task that you tried to hammer out using familiar ideas and techniques. Instead of approaching a problem with familiar concepts, lateral thinking requires that a person explore new and unconventional ideas and perspectives.

Lateral thinking refers to following a path of inquiry that veers off from the more common, predominant path—one that looks for a new angle of entry to a solution. Have you ever tried looking at a different direction by looking harder in the same direction? It doesn't work.

The intersection and lateral thinking models are really two sides of the same coin. Stepping into a stream of intersecting ideas often requires that you step out of old ones. However, in addition to generating new ideas in general, books on the stepping out model often specifically refer to it as a process for problem solving, especially solving nonlinear problems where logical deduction must be bypassed in order to find a solution. Mathematician and researcher David Perkins refers to these types of problems as *rompecabezas*, which in Spanish means *head breakers*. He presents the following example.

> Someone brings an old coin to a museum director and offers it for sale. The coin is stamped "540 B.C.E." Instead of considering the purchase, the museum director calls the police. Why?[5]

By stepping into the intersection, you may be able to think of several possible reasons why the museum director called the police. But lateral thinking emphasizes stepping out of your dominant stream of thought and wading through these possibilities in order to find solutions that break through your common perceptions. Such a solution will not initially be apparent and provides an *aha* moment of clarity similar to the *haha* moments of understanding the punch line to a joke. In the case of this coin *rompecabeza*, a cognitive snap of clarity may occur when you realize that any coin made prior to the birth of Christ would not know to reference his birth.

Panning For Gold

Perkins uses the analogy of panning for gold in the Klondike to describe this process. There are seemingly lots of possible solutions to these problems, just as there is a lot of ground to cover in the Klondike.

Also, we often limit what we think is possible due to preconceptions and past experience, just as those panning for gold often limit their exploration to a small area due to past success there. But it is only by thinking beyond our common perceptions that a sculptor can envision a cocker spaniel in a block of wood, the digital designer can debug an elusive design flaw that he was convinced was the fault of the software engineer, or the music elitist can appreciate the poetic lyrics of a little known California jazz singer.

> I like coffee, pizza, and running
> I find mannequins stunning.
> They all remind me of your beauty; they're just right.
> Shall we wang chung tonight?

Granted, that last one may be a challenge, but it is only by venturing out into the unknown that you may find what you currently do not know...even if it concerns possibly learning how to appreciate something that we may fear or have negative reactions to.

Think of a dish you hated but now love, a career switch you feared but now find joy in, or an art form you never understood but now appreciate.

In fact, these types of lateral expeditions can often lead to uncovering the greatest treasures.

Ruminations of the Unconscious Mind

"What about those eureka moments that seemingly come out of nowhere?" asks a creative tourist looking out at the creativity landscape.

Unlike the previous perspectives involving an active process of finding creative ideas and solutions, here unique ideas often arise seemingly without much conscious effort. You've experienced this if you've ever had ideas pop into your head while enjoying a stroll in the park, while in the middle of an unrelated conversation, or while in the private solitude of your tranquil toilet room. This has led to the view that the creative process is a function of the unconscious mind, the cognitive mechanism that is churning in the background of thought.

Though there are those that underestimate the significance of the unconscious to help us formulate new ideas and solutions, it may in fact be more suited for creative insight than the conscious mind because it has no self-censorship and makes no judgments. As a result, ideas are free to recombine with others to form novel associations and unique patterns.

Professor Kenneth Kraft, a Buddhist scholar at Lehigh University, refers to this type of thinking as *water mind*. The idea is that this frame of mind is akin to the clear and reflective properties of water. It refers to the stilling of our conscious thought allowing us to pay more attention to our unconscious mind.

Guy Claxton, professor of Learning Sciences at the University Of Bristol Graduate School Of Education, refers to the unconscious as the tortoise mind. He makes a distinction between three different speeds of mind.

1. *Faster than thought:* referring to the instantaneous reactions to environmental stimuli our brain and body make in order to keep us alive.
2. *Speed of thought:* corresponding to our conscious thinking, such as when we are deliberating, weighing pros and cons, and constructing arguments.
3. *Tortoise mind:* referring to when we are contemplative or dreamy, think more leisurely, have less purposeful and clear-cut thoughts, and are tolerant of ambiguous information.

Incubation

In creativity texts, the unconscious mind is often associated with the incubation stage of the creative process. This is the period when the conscious mind no longer attacks a problem or attempts to will its way to a new idea. Rather, having done these things, the tortoise mind is allowed to simply incubate. It is what occurs when you "sleep on" a problem in order to solve it. Complex mental processing occurs without your conscious control, below your awareness, just like how your kids are messing around when you aren't looking.

American poet Amy Lowell provides an example of how incubation was key to writing her poem, *The Bronze Horses*. After having thought that horses would make a great subject of a poem, Lowell simply let the idea go. Rather than consciously work on the poem, she simply filed it away in her unconscious. "Six months later, the words of the poem began to come into my head; the poem—to use my private vocabulary—was 'there.'"

Befriending the Tortoise Mind

One of the key points of this tortoise mind view of the creative process is that we must provide it with space and time to do its work.

Orit Gadiesh heads Bain & Company, one of the world's leading strategy consulting firms. She is well respected in her field and is well known for her ingenuity. According to her, in order to be successful, "You have to be willing to 'waste time' on things that are not directly relevant to your work because you are curious. But then you are able to, sometimes unconsciously, integrate them back into your work."[6]

Yet, as anyone who has had sudden insight knows, sometimes the incubation period is not months, days, nor hours. The jazz musician must seemingly access their tortoise mind instantaneously when improvising during a jam session. The improvisational comedian can often come up with new material on the spur of the moment based off of audience interaction.

Creative improvisation is dependent on three main factors that we will continue to discuss in detail throughout the book.

1. Hard work and perseverance: For creativity to flow in an immediate fashion, the jazz musician, the comedian, and any other creative person has to have practiced their craft and practiced improvising—that is, practiced being creative.

2. Joy in the endeavor: As psychology professor Mihaly Csikszentmihalyi notes in his book *Creativity*, the ability to tap into the creative well of the subconscious is very much dependent on one's enjoyment of their endeavor.[7] The more fun we are having in our endeavor, the more conducive we will be to creative manifestations.

3. Being at ease: You must be at ease and trust the flow of the creative, associative process—something creative geniuses, such as Einstein and Leonardo da Vinci, were well known for doing. If we worry or place pressure or expectations on ourselves, we can inhibit our access to creative ideas.

For this last reason, in order for creativity to foster, we need to enter into a relationship with the subconscious mind, where it is allowed to reveal itself on its own terms rather than on the terms we consciously place on it.

In other words, you can't tell the subconscious what to do. Rather, you have to listen to what it is telling you.

The details for how this all works can be found in Chapter 14. But you can begin to get a sense of this by simply taking a few deep breaths and by letting go of the need to get anywhere or achieve anything. This is the only way to clear enough mental space to become aware of what your subconscious has to offer.

You'll be pleasantly surprised by the goodies you'll find after doing some mental spring-cleaning.

The Altered Mind

Have you ever been drunk?

How about high?

If you have, you may recall how your awareness was changed at the time. The world and your experience of it altered in some way, and you may have found yourself immersed in some very unusual thoughts (pink, polka-dotted, three-legged hippos perhaps). This is true whether you have been drunk on love, high on life, or if your mind was altered by some other means that you may be reluctant to divulge.

It does appear that, in order to participate in the creative processes, we must alter how we most commonly use our minds. Either we think differently, laterally, and outside the box, or we have to access the part of our mind that is beneath our conscious awareness. Either way, it seems as if we have to alter the way we think or access our thoughts. This has often been a point of reference for those that look upon creativity as being somehow related to mental illness, or the use of brain-altering substances. The latter was even the subject of a poem by Thomas Moore.

> If with water you fill up your glasses
> You'll never write anything wise;
> For wine is the horse of Parnassus
> That carries the bard to the skies.

Drugs, Alcohol, and the Creative Process

Substances such as these have often been used to either create random associations or to lessen the grips of old ones. Jazz saxophone great Charlie Parker was notorious for performing while on heroin. Guitarist Jimi Hendrix and comedian John Belushi both used drugs at the height of their creative careers. And French painter Maurice Utrillo was known to have painted incredible pictures of Paris while intoxicated.

However, the deaths of Parker, Hendrix and Belushi were all related to their substance abuse. What is more, as his drinking continued, the quality of Utrillo's paintings began to decline, and the end of his life was marked by "attacks of delirium tremens with horrible agitation and terrifying hallucinations."[8]

Even David Crosby, from the musical group Crosby, Stills and Nash, found that drugs did his creative process more harm than good.

> What initially happens in the drug experience is that you feel the drugs helping because they will throw your consciousness up for grabs. And sometimes, early on in the process, that worked for me. The problem with drugs is, as you become addicted to them, they become so debilitating that the creative process stops entirely. [9]

Though the risks of using drugs and alcohol seem to outweigh the rewards, their effects on perception is undeniable. They do change the way we see the world, if only for fleeting moments. In some cultures, many indigenous, this is used to great effect providing its members with a tool to experience an altered perception of reality.

However, without a strong support group or community to provide us with a safe environment and structure for using these substances, we can find ourselves astray in any number of ways. For one, we can fall prey to substance abuse, using it out of habit rather than conscious volition. And another, without the context provided by a community, we can easily fall out of touch with the meaning associated with taking such things. Rather than use them for some transformative purpose, we may simply end up using them because of the addiction to the sensation and feelings that they evoke.

Creativity and Mental Illness

Professor of psychiatry Nancy Andreasen notes that recent films, such as Shine and A Beautiful Mind, have spotlighted mental illness and creativity. The number of creative individuals who have suffered some form of mental illness is numerous. It includes Isaac Newton, Friedrich Nietzsche, Leo Tolstoy, Jonathan Swift, and Robert Schumann to name a few. [10]

Andreasen points to two reasons why mental illness may seem to enhance the creative process. First, many illnesses, such as schizophrenia, are known to disorganize thoughts. This allows novel associations of ideas to come to the forefront. Second, many illnesses inhibit the brain's filtering system, allowing more stimuli to enter into our conscious awareness than usual.

However, the cost of this apparent creativity is great, as it hampers one's capacity to function in the world. The inability to filter unnecessary stimuli makes it difficult to maintain focus, and this obstructs the performance of simple tasks and routine functions. Those with the inability to self-organize their thoughts form psychoses and are prone to delusions. Not only can this make it difficult to complete tasks, but it also can negatively affect their relationships with other people.

The Unaltered Mind

In 1961, in a Manhattan apartment, young Harvard psychologist Timothy Leary was conducting a scientific experiment with a new drug that he claimed would spur on the creative process. It was called psilocybin, which is a key component in magic mushrooms. The apartment was full of poets and writers, including Jack Kerouac. While Kerouac was under the influence of the drug, Leary gave him a paper and pencil, expecting Kerouac to write something extraordinarily creative. Kerouac attempted to comply, but he was only able to draw a few simple lines and laugh nervously—something that I do frequently without the use of mushrooms, magic, or otherwise.

Though there have been creative individuals with mental illness, or who have used substances to enhance their creativity, there is no evidence to show that these are *necessary* traits of the creative process. The association between these traits and creativity seem to stand out because they are popularized by movies, such as *Shine*, or by the attention placed on famous artists who suffer from substance abuse.

There are numerous examples of artists that turn this misperception on its head. Eugene O'Neill is often thought of as a writer whose creativity was at its height when he was drunk. Yet O'Neill has said, "You've got to have all your critical and creative faculties about you when you're working. I never try to write a line when I'm not strictly on the wagon." In contrast to popular belief, it was only after getting sober that he wrote some of his most famous plays, *Morning Becomes Electra, The Iceman Cometh*, and *The Long Day's Journey into Night*.

While mental illness and mind-altering substances can loosen one's preconceptions and expose one to a wider range of sensory stimuli, it can also drastically reduce the ability to function effectively in society. In exchange for more awareness of possibilities and alternative viewpoints, the person with the altered mind may deal with the inability to re-integrate his ideas into a coherent, consistent picture of reality. In his book *Creating from the Spirit*, Dan Wakefield suggests that this inability to perceive a coherent reality may make the users of mind-altering substances ignorant of the truth of their own creative process.

> The deadly idea of alcohol and drugs as glamorous keys to creativity runs through our whole society.... There is a genuine reason for the confusion about alcohol and creativity: the craving for the bottled spirits can mask the need for *spirit*, the source of creation. [11]

There are many ways to alter your thoughts, whether by listening to music, watching TV, relaxing, reading a new magazine, going out for a run, looking at a piece of art, lying down on the floor, stepping into the intersection, stepping out of the stream, dancing, spinning around a room, finding reason to agree with everyone you disagree with and vice versa, or by looking for the humorous side of everything anyone has to say.

Creativity is about discovering more possibilities. How many more ways can you think of to alter your own thoughts?

Releasing the Creative Spirit

In the above quote, Wakefield makes reference to yet another way of articulating the creative process—as a process having to do with the unleashing of spirit.

Let's recall the earlier observation that some ideas seem to come out of nowhere without much conscious effort. One creative tourist points to the unconscious mind as the reason for this. Though, within the context of spirit, another explains this phenomenon as divine inspiration or sourcing creative ideas from some place sacred.

> All of us are endowed with spirit—which means that all of us are naturally creative. We wouldn't exist without the creative force, whose power is acknowledged and dramatized by the first story in the Bible, the creation story…"In the beginning, God created the heavens and the earth." [12]

Prior to the Enlightenment, almost all scientific discoveries, inventions, and art were attributed to the divine or described as being divinely inspired. Even in our modern period, many frame their creative process in these terms. Russian composer Sofia Gubaidulina believes that art is a means to express something greater than oneself and approaches her compositions with the goal of forming a connection to God. Legendary jazz saxophone player and composer John Coltrane refers to his music as the spiritual expression of his being.

Spiritual Descriptions of the Creative Process

- In her book *The Artists Way*, Julia Cameron describes the creative process as the aligning with the creative energy of the universe. She terms this process "spiritual chiropractic."[13] To her, aligning with the creative energy of the universe allows the natural order of life—which is creativity—to flow openly through a person.

- Cameron also asserts that being open to creativity is equivalent to being open to the creativity of the Creator. This is a sentiment shared by opera composer Giacomo Puccini. In describing the creative process of composing his opera, *Madame Butterfly*, Puccini has said, "It was dictated to me by God; I was merely instrumental in putting it on paper and communicating it to the public."

- Dan Wakefield writes extensively of this process in his book *Creating Spirit*. In particular, he emphasizes that all of us are capable of releasing this creative energy. He asserts that the reason many feel encumbered by the creative process is that they are stifled by preconceptions, negative behaviors, and life's usual distractions. As a result, many of us fall into a spiritual sleep. In general, in order to wake up from this slumber, we must empty ourselves of our preconceptions and habits in order make room for the creative spirit.

- Artist and shamanic practitioner Tom Crockett frames this process in indigenous terms. He describes this channeling of the creative spirit as forming a connection between the artist and the "spirit that resides deep in our ancestral memory."[14] In this context, being creative is the sacred act of manifesting the divine breath into material forms, such as words, images, music, and dance.

Getting in Touch with the Creative Spirit

Within this indigenous context, Crockett describes many ways to get in touch with this creative spirit. For example, he advocates entering into a relationship with the soul of all material things. By doing so, he asserts that our perception of spirit in all material things will become clearer. Secondly, he points to dreams as a realm in which we can access the creative spirit, noting that many artists create works based on their dreams and dream imagery.

He also recommends the self-induced trance known as *shamanic journeying* as a method of accessing the creative spirit. The trance is meant to place the individual into a realm somewhere between normal consciousness and the unconscious and can be induced by various practices including meditation, visualization, bodywork, and by altering breathing patterns. Listening to the continuous rhythmic patterns of drums also induces this state of consciousness—a process known as rhythmic entrainment.

However, all major spiritual paths have various methods of getting in touch with the sacred. This could be through praying, through open conversations with the divine, through unselfish acts for others, or through doing one's tasks for a higher power. From this perspective, the creative process is always accessible to us, if we are only humble enough to receive it.

Comparing the Creative Processes

The description of the creative process as the *releasing of the creative spirit* shares many similarities with the other perspectives discussed so far. It points to an emptying out of old ways reminiscent of *stepping out of the stream*. It describes the creative spirit as coming not from the conscious mind, but from somewhere beneath or beyond it, similar to how novel associations seemed to manifest out of the blue from the unconscious mind. Furthermore, accessing the creative spirit through activities such as meditation, prayer, dreaming, and shamanic journeying places the individual into altered states of mind but without the drastic handicaps of the mentally ill or some of the self-imposed handicaps of those who take mind-altering substances.

Now some of you may have cringed throughout this discussion as if talk of spirit and divinity were equivalent to some icky goo that you were afraid to get on your clothes. Or perhaps, some of you were overjoyed by its inclusion in this description of the creative landscape.

In either case, I call your attention to your initial impressions. What were your initial judgments? How did you interpret the language used here? How locked in are you to these interpretations? For the sake of creativity, you may see if you can't find alternative meanings. If you took these words literally, you may want to see how meaningful a metaphorical interpretation can be.

The Helmholz Model

By far, the most popular way of articulating the creative process in psychology texts is the Helmholz model. Though it has no relation to the Heimlich, when you're in a bind, this four-step process just may help you cough up some new ideas.

1. Preparation: It is in this stage that we do the groundwork to learn all we can about the problem that we are trying to find a creative solution for.

2. Incubation: As I have mentioned earlier, it is during this phase, after we have done our due diligence to think consciously and work through our dilemma, that we let our subconscious mind ruminate. This is where we let go of trying to find an answer and just wait patiently for it to arise in our awareness on its own terms.

3. Illumination: It is in this phase that possible solutions and unique ideas bubble up to the surface of our consciousness.

4. Verification: Finally, we take the possible solutions that appear through the illumination phase and test them. We poke and prod them to see if they are useful to us.

It can be very useful to think of the creative process as an easily graspable formulation of phases. To the creativity tourists in the observation tower, thinking this way of creativity makes it seem less daunting and more of an accessible undertaking.

Neuroscience: Activating Unique Neural Networks

From a biological point of view, the organ that is most praised for its involvement in our thought processes is the brain. Oddly enough though, its mention in creativity texts is usually only limited to some general stereotype of the two brain hemispheres. The right is most often gushed over as the creative side, while the left is often referred to as the seat of our robotic, rational tendencies—as if it were a black and white issue. There are definite scientific reasons why popular culture tends to think of the brain hemispheres in this way, but as we'll explore later, the whole brain is critical for creativity.

So in order to get a good look at creativity from neuroscientific perspective, we need to go beyond just the general left-right talk and delve deeper into this spongy, contorted, walnut looking organ that we call the brain.

Complex and Diverse

Imagine the most complex thing you've ever set your eyes or hands on: a car, a rocket ship, the Internet, your home entertainment system, or your mother's meatloaf perhaps. The brain is more complex than any of these. And it isn't even close.

The brain is Mother Nature's David. It's the crème de la crème of ingenuity and invention. For the sake of simplicity, you can think of it as consisting of three major physical layers. The first layer is the part of the brain that regulates our heart rate, breathing, and our levels of wakefulness and sleep among other things. And as most of you have already experienced, it does this without our conscious effort. It does it automatically.

On top of this is a second layer that is responsible for controlling our body temperature, blood sugar levels, blood pressure, and hormone levels. This layer is also responsible for the famous 4 F's: feeding, fornicating, and the flight-or-fight stress response. Feeding refers to the drive to find food and feed ourselves. The flight-or-fight response refers to our response to potentially dangerous situations. So when we find ourselves threatened by a wild bear, this second layer of the brain kicks in, and we either run or prepare to duke it out—though nowadays it often gets activated by our boss's evil eye or by our latest mortgage bill. Lastly, fornicating refers to our impulse to listen to Barry White music...in a manner of speaking. And again, though we can have a conscious effect on these things, our brain performs all these tasks too below our conscious awareness.

Where humans and other highly developed mammals differ from

other creatures is in the development of a third layer known as the cerebrum, neocortex, or new brain. This is the Nerf-football-looking gray mass that most of us envision when we think of the brain. It is this third layer that is split down the middle into two halves called hemispheres.

Each hemisphere is comprised of four major sections called lobes that are critical for specific functions. These lobes are the hub of activity for processing specialized information. They are like the A-Team, each with their own specialty that enables us to function as a whole. For example, one lobe is heavily involved in processing visual information, another in processing audible information, and yet another is critical for planning.

To recap: Three major layers…the third split into two major halves, each with four sections…an organ that keeps track of a whole mess of bodily functions simultaneously, mostly underneath our conscious awareness….

Sitting on top of our bodies, behind our eyes is the most advanced technology ever invented and the most creative work of art ever manifested—molded out of the same stuff that forms the stars in the sky and the ground beneath our feet. And unlike just about anything else in our possession, you truly can't leave home without it…not that I've tried.

Commonalities

Like a great metropolitan city, the brain is always buzzing with activity due to its diversity in anatomy and functionality. Yet, amongst this diversity exist two crucial commonalities that are of great importance to our discussion of creativity.

1. While each of the lobes is thought of as specialized in some way, they each also have sections that are unspecialized. It is through this area, known as the association cortex, that different specialized sections of the brain are linked and associated. It's like having the financial center of town also including a section of folks whose job is to connect the financial center to the restaurant area or the shopping district. This unspecialized section may not be intimately involved in the finances, but they're critical in connecting the financial center to all other areas of the city.

2. The entire human brain is comprised of trillions of brain cells called neurons. In one respect, you can think of the neurons as the people in the city. However, each of these neurons is typically linked to up to 10,000 other neurons in a vast neural network—like a spider web or a chain-linked fence. So the more popular analogy is to think of these neurons as computers within a vast communication network, since each neuron is in constant communication with clusters of other neurons. Each neuron can send only one of two signals to each other. They can either send a signal that urges other neurons to fire signals to others (shoot already!), or they can send one that suppresses such firings (don't shoot!). It is through this type of communication that the different areas of the brain speak to one another.

Creativity

Every time we feel, sense, see, think, speak, or decide to move our bodies, there is a unique activation of neural firing patterns; a particular web or chain of neurons is triggered, each communicating a signal to others in its chain like in a game of telephone.

For example, if we see an apple, one pattern may be activated, whereas if we hear a dog barking, another pattern of neurons is activated. Figure 3 below is a very, very generalized visual analogy of this.

Figure 3

Neural firing pattern when we see an apple.

Neural firing pattern when we hear a dog.

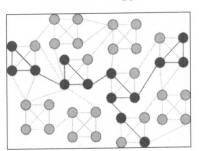 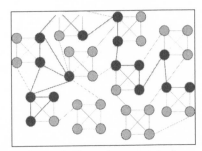

In a very general sense then, thinking differently—creatively—means activating a unique network of neurons. It means that when we look at a blank canvas or are pondering a dilemma, we find a way to trigger a particular web that we had not triggered before. It means stimulating a new chain and forming novel associations between neurons.

Hmm....novel associations...sounds familiar?

Understanding how the brain operates reveals a wealth of insights about the creative process, some that are often looked upon as beyond the realm of science. It has some very interesting implications for the validity of epiphanies; for how we should be educating our children; for how to foster creative environments; for the significance of mythology, religion, and poetry; as well as for how we can live lives that are more creative.

The neurological description you have just read is a brief summary of a pretty complicated framework. Fortunately, these ideas get fleshed out in great detail in the chapters to come.

It is this neurological framework that provides the foundation for the remainder of this book.

Summary from the Observation Tower: The Elephant in the Dark

For much of my creative research, I was stumbling around in the dark, exploring different aspects of the creative process. It was akin to the allegory of the blind men and the elephant. Each man perceived the elephant to be whatever part they were able to experience—a hosepipe for those feeling its trunk, a large fan for those feeling its ear, or a pillar for those feeling its leg.

In this same way, some experience the creative process as hard work and luck, while some believe it to be intersecting streams of ideas and perspectives. Some articulate it as removing oneself from ingrained beliefs and habits, while others see it as a four-step process. Yet others think of it primarily as the ruminations of the unconscious mind or the unleashing of the creative spirit.

By exposing you to these various perspectives of the creative process, I wanted to share the different ways that it is often spoken of in popular culture, taught in seminars, and written about in creative thinking books. Each perspective is useful, and with each analogy, we are given a unique way to identify with the process of thinking differently.

But now, with the help of cognitive science, I want to shed light on a new analogy, one that helped me constellate all the perspectives we have reviewed thus far. Just as the description of a 4-step process has provided many with an easily graspable framework for creative endeavors, it can be useful to have an understanding of what the creative process entails. It can be helpful to have some sort of a guide to help us contextualize what we feel and what we face as we try to think differently—an analogy or map that makes it easier to identify where we are in the creative process, the obstacles that often stymie the process, and the actions needed to transcend these obstacles in order to continue our creative undertakings.

How can any of us look at the same thing and see completely different things—intersecting streams, hard work, unconscious mind, and spirit?

These questions are at the heart of *Part II—How: The Creative Journey*. And there's a completely reasonable explanation for this.

By delving into the depths of neuroscience, we will investigate how we commonly think, why we commonly think that way, and how we can learn to think differently. What we will soon find out is that our sense of reason is often unreasonable. We will discover that it is only by deviating from our common sense that we can gain not just a more creative perspective, but also a more complete one.

This will all become clearer as we come down from our observation tower, tighten up our shoelaces, and begin to actually journey through the adventurous terrain of the creative landscape.

PART II
How: The Creative Journey

The 1st Aspect
The Ordinary World

What Lies Beyond The Shore?

A giggle could be heard, then a laugh. And the villagers looked at each other wondering who was laughing at a time like this.

"Foolish villagers," said the beggar.

The villagers looked upon the ground, finally noticing the beggar who seemed to blend in with the brown dirt and brown bark of the tree.

"Look at him—poor beggar. He even goes without a proper pickle loincloth and doughnut necklace. What odd rags do you have around your legs?"

"These are tight leather pants and my blouse is thin chiffon," the beggar replied.

"Who has heard of such foolish things? You must be a cursed soul."

"Yes I am," he said. "As you too will be if you fail to listen to me."

"And what do you know of such things, beggar?"

"I know these things very well."

"Nonsense! Look at you," questioned the laborer. "You are simply a beggar. If you knew such things, you'd be more."

"I wasn't always a beggar, my pickle picking friend. I was once an explorer."

The doughnut maker was stunned. "An explorer? Of which part of the island?"

"Not within the island, my doughnut hole punching compadre. I was an explorer outside of the island."

"Outside of the island?" They all were flabbergasted at the notion, for they all knew that there was nothing outside of the island.

"There is nothing outside of the island!"

"How do you know?" asked the beggar.

"How do I know? I can see with my own two eyes," replied the religious person.

"You have seen? Have you ever ventured beyond our shores?"

"Why in the world would I do such a thing?" the chef answered. "You need only walk along the coast around the island, and you can plainly see that there is nothing beyond our shores but endless seas."

"You think you see completely? You cannot even agree on what you saw at the carnival, and yet you are certain of what exists outside our island without stepping one foot outside it."

The villagers stood on their toes trying to see beyond the shore.

"I can offer you a way to resolve your differences, to find unique solutions to the dilemmas that brought you to this carnival in the first place. You see, on another island, beyond what the eye can see, there exists hidden treasure."

"Treasure!" exclaimed all the villagers.

"Yes. See this oak tree? With this treasure, you will be able to take this tree and use it to build your huts, your work tools…you will be able to use it for the arts and musical instruments."

"Are you saying we can turn that tree into a giant pickle?"

"No."

"Into a giant doughnut?"

"No…take a look at the carnival behind you. After you find this treasure, you will have a better understanding of what the barkers were selling and how to use their various products. But more than this, you will become aware that the carnival used more than pickles and doughnuts to build their tents, set up their stages, prepare their foods, and feed their assortment of entertainers."

The villagers looked back and watched the tents fall. They watched as the carnival workers packed up their equipment. But all the villagers could see were strangely constructed doughnut canvases, strong pickle poles, and other miscellaneously fantastic pickle-doughnut materials.

"That makes no sense!" yelled the chef. "It is obviously only pickles and doughnuts. That's all there is. It is a common fact.

Everyone knows that."

The beggar added calmly, "After finding the treasure, you will come to realize that your common sense is limiting your access to possibilities."

"But nobody travels beyond the shore. It is much too dangerous."

"Much too scary."

"You must be mad!"

"No. Not mad...just a little different," the beggar said with a gentle smile. "In order for you to find what you seek, you must first realize that there is more to the world than this island. You must see that what you see may not be what everyone else sees. And you must recognize that all great ideas, at their point of conception, defied *common* sensibilities—that's what made them great."

CHAPTER THREE
Origins of Our Ordinary World: The Science of Visual Perception

Congratulations on beginning your adventure through the creative landscape. To truly embark on our exploration of the creative process, we will first try to understand the workings of our common sensibilities. Your journey may get bumpy, but a little turbulence never hurt anyone, right? It just may be what you need to stir up your latest creative cocktails.

Where do we start?

Let us recall the mental metropolis analogy from the previous chapter. If each neuron is like a person in the city, then every time we have a thought certain groups of our citizens start talking to each other. It's sort of like when you tell your Aunt Mathilda that you found an odd shaped mole on your rear. Before you can blink, the whole family is asking you about it, but luckily for you, your coworkers aren't on that network.

By investigating the attributes and structures of these neural networks, we can begin to achieve a better understanding of our more common thought processes; we can get a better grasp of how common sensibilities work.

The easiest way to dive into this is by first looking at our visual perception. Then in the next chapter, we will expand our exploration to other cognitive processes. What we will discover is that our common sense tends to oversimplify the world and, as a result, limits our access to creative possibilities.

Why We Only See Pickles and Doughnuts

Have you ever been at a store and mistook the back of somebody's head for another person?

It's not too bad when you're thinking they're your accountant or real estate agent, but it's kind of embarrassing when you begin to wrap your arms around a total stranger thinking they're your spouse...very awkward. How are you going to explain that one?

Just looked like you needed a hug today?
...I'm a member of the Humanitarian Hugging Society?

I don't think so.

We often take our perception of the world for granted. We rarely doubt if what we perceive through our major senses (sight, sound, taste, touch, and smell) is exactly how the world exists outside of our bodies. Most of us carry the intuitive notion that the appearance of the external word is somehow captured through our eyes and replicated on a screen in our brains that we perceive in its totality.

Figure 4

But our experience of the world does not come directly into our awareness untouched. When we look at the image of an apple in Figure 4, light reflects off the image and strikes various cells in our retina, located at the back of the eye. The light photons then stimulate electrical nerve impulses that travel the eye's neural pathways to the lobe in our brain that specializes in visual processing. From here, neurons in other parts of our brain are triggered in order to further interpret the visual stimuli.

Mumbo jumbo, chaumba wuamba, pathway nap away...so what does it all mean?

What this means is that our visual perception of reality is not absolute and purely objective. What we see isn't just dependent on the apple in front of us. What we see is filtered, dependent on the integrity of our visual pathways, and shaped by the pre-existing constructs of our brain.

Think of how television works. In a studio somewhere, a scene is shot and captured on film. The images on the film must somehow be processed into data that can be sent over the airwaves or through cable, and then your television must receive and process this data to display the image on your screen.

What you see on the screen is then not solely dependent on the scene that was shot, but also dependent on all the stuff going on before it reaches you and your bag of potato chips. If there is a storm, the signal reaching your magic box may be noisy and distort the image on your screen. Or imagine what happens in your house when your television settings for tint, color, or sharpness are different from one room to the next. To you, watching in the bedroom, Alex Trebek may appear pale, but to your husband watching in another room, he may look downright pasty.

Just as what you see on the television is affected by the television itself, your visual perception of the external world is affected by your brain's internal structures—by how your neurons are wired together.

What You See Isn't Necessarily What You Get

Are you saying that when a group of us are looking at the same object, we may perceive it differently?

Yes. Intuitively, we are aware of this notion. There are many people who are affected by brain damage, or who are colorblind, or who require glasses to see clearly. Their perception of an apple can be very different from yours. It isn't necessarily that the world is different for each of us, but that we all perceive it differently. Though we often think we see the world unobstructed, it always is—by our eyes, our optical pathways, and our brains.

Don't I experience the world pretty much as it is? It feels like my perception is pretty much right on, and whatever inaccuracy may exist is unnoticeable.

It may feel that way. But take a look at the images below. They are often used to demonstrate how our internal neural structures play as much, if not more, of a role in our visual perception than the object of perception itself.

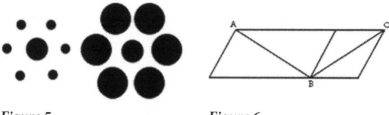

Figure 5   **Figure 6**

In Figure 5, compare the sizes of the two center circles. Does one seem smaller than the other? If you're like most, the left center circle will appear larger than the right.

In Figure 6, compare the sizes of the two diagonal lines, A-B and B-C. Does one seem longer than the other? For many, line A-B will appear longer than B-C.

In actuality, if you were to take a ruler and measure the sizes of the inner circles in Figure 5, you would discover that they are the same size. Similarly, lines A-B and C-B in Figure 6 are of equal length. As you see (or may not see), our visual perception of the images in Figures 5 and 6 is not absolute.

What?! What's going on here?

As I mentioned before, our visual interpretations are related to our pre-existing neural structures. In particular, what these figures demonstrate is that our neural connections appear to have developed to provide us with a short cut method of visual interpretation with which we can make *quick decisions based off of visual clues and relationships.*

The left center circle in Figure 5 appears larger due to the size of the circles surrounding it in comparison to the right constellation. Lines A-B and C-B in Figure 6 often appear to be of different lengths because of their visual relationship with their neighboring lines. So, instead of seeing objects objectively, we have a tendency to come to conclusions about what we see based on what is around it, how it appears in relation to its environment—based off of context.

These short cut interpretations enabled our ancestors to react swiftly to their environment in order to avoid danger, such as when trying to determine how far away they were from approaching lions, tigers, and bears—*oh my!*—and other predators in their environment.

If Caveman Fred spotted an approaching leopard, there may not be much time to do careful, accurate measurements to determine if the leopard was in range for a kill. Poor Fred may be eaten before completing his measurements. Instead, his brain had developed a quick way of estimating such things. In his environment, it was better to be safe than accurate.

The Big Picture: Visual Pattern Recognition

Okay. So maybe, I get some specifics wrong. But in general, don't I pretty much see the big picture as it is?

Actually, it isn't just that we may get some specifics wrong, but that we often don't even use all the specifics to get a sense of the big picture. Our ability to react efficiently is aided by our ability to make sense out of *limited* information. In other words, we have the capacity to fill in the gaps in our experiences and make judgments with incomplete knowledge. We are experts at coming to a conclusion about what we are seeing without really "seeing" everything.

Figure 7

Do you recognize this to be an apple, though it's only partially visible?

To get a better understanding of how this works, think about this:

Have you ever purchased a certain type of car and, then suddenly, become aware of that particular model on the streets? Or have you started a new activity, like riding a bike, and then suddenly, it seems as if everyone is doing it too?

It's because you have become more prone to be stimulated by those things. Analogously, within our brains, certain interlinked webs of neurons are more prone to be activated than others when encountering particular stimuli. In essence, all the "bike riders" of our mental metropolis get excited over seeing a bike, or all our black BMW neurons get excited over seeing one.

To use an example from our sense of hearing, some dancers may perk up at hearing the dance term *arabesque,** while the rest of us wouldn't care. At most we may think, *huh? Is that edible?*

And just as we may gain the attention of all owners of a black BMW sedan by showing one to them or the attention of all the dancers in the room by yelling out a dance term, certain networks of brain cells can be primed, made more alert and ready to quickly react to the *slightest hint* of the same stimuli were it to come again.

For example, exposing you to the apple in Figure 4 activated a particular neural network in your brain. That experience primed a particular neural network—the one associated with your idea of an "apple"—and made it more susceptible to being activated again with limited information as in the half apple in Figure 7.

In a sense, your "apple" neural web was warmed up, making it fire easily again by just a slight push of limited information. Moreover, this network may have already been sufficiently warmed up by the notion you already had of what an apple looked like even before you saw Figure 4.

This implies that what you perceive is not solely based on what is out there in the world—it is affected by your mental states and the beliefs that you bring to an experience.

What do you see in Figure 8? If you only see black dots, maybe I can influence your perception by influencing your mental states.

Can you see a dog sniffing on the ground, its head in the center of the picture? Take a minute. (Turn the page for a hint.)

Figure 8

---

* It is a position in which the dancer stands on one leg, straight or bent, with the other extended to the back at 90 degrees.

Do you see a white triangle, though the picture only contains three black circles with slices removed from each one?

Depending on how you want to see this figure, can you go back and forth between seeing a white triangle and three Pacmen?

Figure 9

Figure 10

Though these images are in some sense incomplete, our mind is able to organize the available visual information into complete pictures rather than disconnected ones—a *gestalt*.

In short, our mind is wired for visual *pattern recognition*. We are able to recognize parts as fitting within a coherent pattern. Or, to say it differently, our mind takes the pieces it does see and tries to make it fit within a more complete story.

As you saw with the apple example, when the shape, color, form etc. of the object in front of you resemble something you've previously experienced, they activate similar neural firing patterns. As a result, what you see is then associated with what you have seen previously.

Upon seeing an object in the backyard, your mind may say to itself: *hey, this thing is long, dark, skinny, and coiled in the grass just like a snake. Oh no, this must be another snake!*—And hopefully, you'll recognize the object as a snake before it has a chance to attack you. Or, by recognizing the back of your child's haircut, you quickly find her if she gets lost in a crowd.

Snake Bitten By Visual Pattern Recognition

Visual pattern recognition is good, right? I don't want to have to go through my entire "snake checklist" making sure it is what I think it is before reacting to it.

And that's exactly why we developed such a mechanism—in order to make snap judgments and decisions that are key to reacting to life-threatening situations, when time is a premium. Caveman Fred, his cave-wife Wilma, and their cave-baby Pebbles were able to stay alive in threatening environments, in large part, because of these mechanisms.

It is because of our strong interconnections (3ft tall, gold pony tail = Jennifer; black, thin, forked tongue = snake) that we are able to make quick decisions based on visual relationships rather than close inspection. It is also how we are able to fill in the gaps of our perception to make sense of the world and how we can come to conclusions based on limited information.

This also explains how an expert mechanic or computer technician can fix problems faster than novices can. Over time, experts in particular fields have developed such strong associations and familiarity with certain scenarios that they can quickly diagnose what's wrong. They are more efficient and well skilled at pattern recognition within their particular endeavor, just as you are such an expert of your own children that you can recognize them just by their haircut.

Let's say out of the corner of your eye you see something dark, thin, long, and curved. Similar to interpreting the gestalt images presented earlier, you come to a perception—a judgment of what you are seeing—with only this limited information (Figure 11).

Figure 11

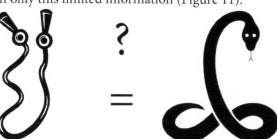

While our quick discernment traits have been beneficial to our survival, our propensity for visual pattern recognition has made us prone to overgeneralizations and susceptible to errors due to our limited, subjective visual perception of the world.

It is for this reason that our hypothetical dancers may think there's some deep dance conversation going on, though people are only talking about "air," "Arabs," or "baskets." Or our black BMW owners may think they see a black BMW from the corner of their eye when in fact it's a black Ford Focus.

But what does this have to do with the ability to think differently?

Reflect back to the gestalt images in Figures 8 and 9. Was it difficult for you to alternate between different perceptions of the images? Often we are more prone to favor one perception over the rest. You can experience this again with the example in Figure 12.

Some see a white vase in the center of a black backdrop. Others see two black silhouettes of two heads facing each other.

By changing what you want to see, can you oscillate between the two interpretations? Are you drawn to one in particular?

Figure 12

One story of how to make sense out of the image is usually stronger than others. In the case of these previous images, it may be easier to perceive alternative interpretations because the alternatives were pointed out to you. But, what if they weren't? Or what if alternatives were pointed out to you only after you had lived your life perceiving only one out of the many interpretations? It can be very difficult to see differently after so much practice in seeing it through the lens of one particular story.

This means that our choices and possibilities are often limited because of the limitations of our perceptions. You may find it difficult to imagine a clump of mud as a delicate figurine, or a hammer as anything but a tool for installing nails, or a rock as being marketable as a pet.* It is because of limited perceptions that our ancestors were convinced that the earth was flat and that the sky obviously rotated around a stationary earth.

Some of the fears and anxieties that you experience may also be due to these overgeneralizations and misperceptions. Think of the fear you may experience when you see somebody that dresses a certain way or has a certain look. Think of the anxiety that you may feel when somebody makes a particular facial expression or hand gesture.

The limitations in perceptions can cause conflicts between individuals who have differing interpretations of what they're looking at. Our snap judgment mechanism may make us feel that we're right when we're actually wrong, as may be the case with the black, thin, coiled object in the grass.

These conflicts can also often occur when no party is wrong, but simply because each interprets the visual stimuli with a different story. For example, one man's symbol of evil could be another's symbol of good, as is the case with the swastika (originally a sacred religious symbol of the east that was later adopted by the Nazis).

The stories we tell ourselves of what we see are then not just imprecise, but can lead to limited perception and unnecessary strife. What science shows is that there is definitely more to the object of our perception than what we see, and what we see is influenced by what our minds are prepared to see—influenced by preexisting beliefs, mental states, and neural structures.

If you're a chess player, you may be more prone to experiencing the world in terms of strategic moves that need to be analyzed. If you're a gambler, you may tend to experience the world in terms of risk and reward. And if you're a parent, you may see the world in terms of your children: is this safe, would my child enjoy that, is this restaurant child friendly or would they throw me out in two seconds, etc…

For you to have a greater perception of possibilities, you have to realize that unless you are in a life-threatening situation that requires

---

* For those who are not familiar with this, it is a reference to the Pet Rock, rocks that were marketed as pets back in the 1970s. It was the brainchild of Gary Dahl and was a fad that made Dahl a millionaire over the span of a few months.

immediate response (and no, choosing the right pair of shoes or deciding on the right tie do not count), you can always look for more than what you are currently seeing. This is true because the same visual faculties that kept our ancestors alive in the wild are the same faculties that cause modern day Fred, Wilma, and Pebbles to jump at the sight of a black jump rope coiled up in the grass of their backyard.

CHAPTER FOUR

Origins of Our Ordinary World (The Sequel): The Science of Common Sense Thinking

In the last chapter, we saw how our visual perception can be incomplete and flawed in some way because it relies on a short cut: pattern recognition. Rather than take time to thoroughly see things as they are, our brains are able to come to quick judgments based on limited information and past experience.

But what about our other cognitive faculties: how we process information, think about scenarios, and solve problems?

To answer this, let's take a look at the following questions:

1. What is the next number in a sequence of 1, 3, 5, 7…?
2. If Ronald McDonald was running toward Colonel Sanders at 10 miles an hour and the Colonel was running toward Ronald at 20 miles an hour, how long would it take for them to pass each other if they started running at the same time, 100 miles apart.*

Pattern recognition helps us solve these problems because we are able to come to quick interpretations of what these questions are asking. It also enables us to recognize these problems as being similar to ones we may have experienced in the past, and hopefully, we can apply the same problem solving techniques with great success.

Pattern recognition is a great tool for doing mathematics, spotting trends, preparing for future occurrences, and other skills often

---

*Although, I don't know any human who can run 20 miles in an hour, much less an older gentleman who uses a cane and sells fried chicken by the bucket.

identified with professional and academic competence. It is also the faculty of mind needed for composing step-by-step instructions for installing a computer network or for assembling your kids' overpriced play set.

However, we get into trouble when we think this is the *only* way to process information. We get into trouble when we think this is the *only* way to get new ideas and solve problems. Just as with our visual perception, we are again prone to overgeneralizations and cognitive difficulties that stem from our short cut mechanisms.

Why We Only Think About Pickles and Doughnuts

Imagine the following scenario: *two men are found dead in their cabin in the woods.*

The description of the scenario triggered a particular chain of neural firings based on how you associate men, death, and woods. In order to understand the scenario, you try to fit it within *that* pre-existing framework.

Now, convert this scenario into a problem: "How did the two men die?" To solve this problem, you are only allowed to ask yes or no questions. Some typical inquiries may include the following: *Did the men know each other? Was murder involved? Was it very cold? Was it very hot? Were they hungry? Were the men gravely sick or very old when they died? Was there an accident?*

Take a moment to think about this scenario yourself. What other questions would you ask? What explanations would cross your mind? Your response to these two questions represents your ordinary pool of ideas and possibilities.

The typical neural network associated with this scenario provides us with our literal, dominant understanding. In other words, the people in our mental metropolis who are most excited when hearing this scenario determine how we interpret it. For some, this may bring about a mental picture of a cozy log cabin nested amongst the trees of a beautiful forest. For you, it may bring about memories of a secret rendezvous with your piano teacher or of the one night you struggled to live without modern plumbing.

This understanding is the pattern that our mind recognizes most easily given the scenario, just as we recognized an apple behind a rectangle in Figure 7 or a coil of black jump rope as a snake. This dominant pattern shapes what we think is possible and limits the scope of our inquiry in order to make us an efficient problem solver.

On the other hand, this narrowing of conceptual space also limits our access to possible solutions. Often, the pattern recognized is so strong that we can have difficulty envisioning an alternative one. This occurs for the same reason that made it difficult to hold alternate interpretations of the images in Figures 8, 9, and 12. One story is more strongly associated with the given attributes of the scenario than any other story. And by story, I mean the meaning we assign, how we make sense of the information given.

In this particular scenario, the two men did not die from disease, starvation, or foul play. Rather, they died as a result of an airplane crash ("dead in their *cabin* in the woods"). If this interpretation is new to you not only does your understanding of the scenario change, but also questions that once seemed valid now seem nonsensical and void of significance. *Were they hungry?*

Upon reading the initial description of the scenario, "two men were found dead in their cabin in the woods," we were propelled to an immediate interpretation of it—propelled to assume a particular story of what it means. This illustrates how pattern recognition can become an automatized response. Unconsciously, our neural networks helped us make sense of the description by attributing meaning through assumptions and inferences. Don't be mad at the people in your mental metropolis. They're just doing their jobs.

Why does my brain rely so much on pattern recognition?

This automatic response reduces our cognitive efforts and reduces the burden placed on our awareness. This is accomplished by simplifying the world of our perception, filling in the missing pieces based upon what we know from past experiences. This is how we are able to perform multiple tasks simultaneously, such as walk and chew gum. It is also how we are simultaneously able to watch TV and eat a meal without choking on a chicken bone. These skills have created such a well-practiced neural pattern that they can be performed while our attention is placed elsewhere. We have become *experts* at these tasks.

Yet it is also because of these ingrained neural patterns that many experts have difficulty thinking outside the box. While they are quickly able to come to conclusions based on limited information, they have difficulty seeing a scenario with "fresh eyes"—like through the eyes of a novice.

Thinking differently can then be defined as activating different neural networks than our automatic ones. This is exactly what happened when we learned that the cabin in the woods referred to the wreckage of an airplane rather than a cozy log cabin. But what we want to develop is the ability to activate different neural networks on our own at will.

Mental Rules of Thumb and Cognitive Illusions

Are you saying a lot of our thinking is based on short cuts?

Exactly! But these are short cuts or rules of thumb that we usually aren't aware we are using. We use them habitually without thinking about it. Just as we used short cuts and rules of thumb in visual perception, we habitually use simple and approximate mental strategies when dealing with certain types of decision making and problem solving.

Mental strategies save us time and energy when compared to performing deductive justifications according to strict logic because they enable us to make snap judgments based on well-recognized clues. These rules of thumb, or *heuristics*, often arise as a pattern response to scenarios that resemble those we have previously encountered. They can help us function in the world more efficiently. But, by virtue of being *simple* and *approximate* rules, they leave us vulnerable to misunderstandings and false concepts, as is the case with visual pattern recognition.

In his book *Inevitable Illusion*, Massimo Piattelli-Palmarini lists many common examples of these misunderstandings and refers to them as cognitive illusions.

Logic Illusions

Have you ever known a guy who always thought they were right and were always convinced of their own rational arguments? The following series of syllogisms (using the fictional "BO University") highlight a cognitive illusion of our sense of logic and rational thinking.[1]

Given the premise:

> All BO University students are educated.
> John is a BO University student.

We can easily come to the following conclusion:

> John is educated.

Given the premise:

> No beautician is a sailor.
> All BO University students are beauticians.

We can logically deduce that:

> No BO University student is a sailor.

However, given the premise:

> All BO University students are criminals.
> No game show hosts are BO University students.

What conclusion can we draw?

Give yourself a moment to really think this through. It may not be as clear-cut as the first two syllogisms.

You may say that *no game show host is a criminal* or that *no criminal is a game show host*. Both are incorrect. Many logic-minded folks may say that no conclusion can be drawn here.

We recognized a pattern in the first two syllogisms—deductive logic based on elimination of possibilities given particular assumptions. The answer in these examples had to be in the form of "this or that, educated or not, beautician or not, but not both."

We imposed this pattern—*vertical thinking* in creativity guru Edward de Bono's terms[2]—on the third syllogism unsuccessfully and were unable to come to any conclusion. Because the pattern we recognized was dualistic—this or that, but not both—we find it difficult to think of possible inclusive solutions: *"Some" criminals are not BO University students or "some" criminals are not game show hosts.*

This cognitive illusion illustrates how our strong sense of reason can be fallible. Unnecessary bickering and tension can occur within groups or within our own heads when one voice seems absolutely certain of its position. Just reflect on the last argument you had with a coworker, friend, acquaintance, or national leader (for my readers who are heads of states). This arrogance not only causes unnecessary friction that slows the creative process, but it can also convince us to shut out possibilities and alternatives that may be equally valid. And with the example above, our sense of reason prohibited us from seeing *any* possibilities as valid.

Framing Illusions

Have you ever wondered why advertisers are so good at selling a rotten idea or a crummy product to the public? As you're probably already aware, part of the answer is how they frame it. Studies have shown that our decisions are affected by how a scenario is framed as opposed to the strict facts about the situation.

> In a survey, when clinicians were told that the mortality rate for a certain operation is 7 percent within 5 years, they hesitated to recommend it. On the other hand, when they were told it had a survival rate of 93 percent after 5 years, they were more inclined to recommend it to their patients.[3]

Look closely at both cases. The facts presented in both were exactly the same. Nevertheless, framing the information with the words "survival rate" triggered a more favorable story than the words "mortality rate." These particular words were so strongly tied to certain perceptions that some clinicians came to conclusions without thinking through the information. This illusion parallels the visual illusions of circles and lines illustrated in Figures 5 and 6 where our perceptions of size were based on the contextual elements.

Advertisers use this to their advantage. Think of how different companies sell us the exact same products, but because of how the product is framed, one brand seems more appealing than the other. Are designer jeans from a fancy department store really hundreds of dollars better than a similar pair without the cache? Is named brand toilet paper really that much better than the generic brand? Our perceptions of what is good and bad or of what is correct and incorrect can be faulty or incomplete because of the context of our experience.

More to the point, imagine being stuck while trying to complete a new painting, book, song; while developing a new invention; or while trying to solve a problem. Our moods can swing from depression and despair, to hope and excitement just based on how we look at our situation. By framing our predicament as hopeless, we lose all energy to move forward. If we frame it as a hopeful process, we may find inspiration to go beyond our "normal" capacities. It is totally up to us how we frame it. It's our choice whether to see it as a Creative Journey or a meaningless, mundane task.

The choice is ours once we realize we have the option to think differently.

Probability Illusions

Try and reflect on the last decision you made or one that you have to make soon. Maybe, you were deciding on what to wear this morning. Maybe, you are thinking about taking on a new career. Maybe, you were deciding on when to put in some time on your next work of art or invention. Or perhaps the last decision you made was simply to continue reading this section though you may have been apprehensive that "probability illusions" could mean doing lots of math.

Nobody ever really knows what will happen next, but we often take guesses so that we can proceed with our lives. We guess as to what the weather might be throughout the day or what that cute guy or gal at the coffee shop would think of our outfit. We guess as to how happy or miserable we may be with a career move or how difficult it may be to do it. We may guess what the chances are people will actually like our art or invention. Or you may have taken a chance with this section assuming there wouldn't be any real math since there hasn't been any up to this point.

Just as with logic and framing illusions, we very often have cognitive illusions concerning the likelihood of something happening. This can be problematic because we base so many of our actions and decisions on our perception of probabilities.

1. HHHHTTT
2. THHTHTT
3. TTTTTTT

Given 7 consecutive and independent coin flips, which scenario to the left do you think is most likely? Most would say that #2 is most likely, followed by #1, then #3. Actually, the math says that each scenario is of equal probability.[4]

Figure 13

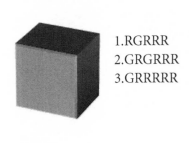

1.RGRRR
2.GRGRRR
3.GRRRRR

Figure 14

Given consecutive and independent rolls of a normal die with four faces died red and two faces died green, which scenario to the left do you think is most likely? Most would place the order of likelihood beginning with #2, followed by #1, followed by #3. Yet the actual order in descending likelihood is #1, #3, and then #2.[5]

Both Figures 13 and 14 illustrate that we often perceive the probability of a situation with a heuristic of *typicality* rather than by using precise probability calculations. In the scenario described in Figure 13, outcome #2 seems to have a more balanced frequency of heads and tails. This balanced frequency is what we may *typically* expect based on experience or on some understanding of 50/50 probabilities and randomness. However, since heads and tails have the same probability of occurrence, all possible outcomes given the same number of flips are equally likely.

I can hear the math geeks flipping to the endnotes to see how this works.

Similarly, in the scenario described in Figure 14, outcome #2 seems to have a more balanced occurrence of red and green though outcome #1 has the higher mathematical probability of occurrence. Further, unlike flipping a coin, because the probabilities of red and green rolls of the die are unequal, an outcome with all reds (RRRRR for example with five rolls) is always most likely.

Do I need to understand all of this probability theory?

It's not necessary to get the math. The important part is to remember that what seems most probable to us may be more typical according to our experience but isn't necessarily more probable.

This heuristic of *typicality* is what we often base our decisions on. Yet not only can this short cut rule of thumb lead to many wrongly biased decisions as illustrated in Figures 13 and 14, but it is also often a key source of depression, fear, and frustration. Over time, the human brain has developed the capacity for abstract thought, and that has provided us with the capability to think through scenarios before acting upon them. We have developed an ability to hypothesize about the future. And this ability to hypothesize about the future has led to the propensity to worry and fear possible scenarios that may or may not occur.

If we were to realize that these scenarios are not certainties, and may even be unlikely, it may be possible to alleviate some of our mental anguish. However, because of our propensity to use a heuristic of typicality, we can find ourselves worrying excessively about finding a mate simply because we have not found one yet, or we may be fraught with the fear of losing a girlfriend because we have experienced breakups in the past and we may feel that our relationship is *due* for one.

Hopefully, you now have a better sense of why our common modes of thinking can often put us in a bind. They constrict our perceptions and our access to alternatives. They can cause problems in groups when people don't agree on how to interpret information or on how to view a particular scenario. As a result, there may be conflict when trying to create and implement solutions to problems or when trying to arrive at an optimal path or product.

But overall, my general perceptions seem to work just fine. They seem good enough for what I do day in and day out.

For the most part, that may be true. But if we're looking to create something new or discover alternative courses of action, our general perceptions will need to shift. In order to think creatively, we'll have to work through the inaccuracies in our perception and work past our limited way of thinking.

Additionally, if you ever get frustrated, anxious, fearful, depressed, stuck, or angry about the problems you face or about your particular circumstances, that may be an indication that your experience isn't jiving with your assumptions. You may want to consider re-evaluating *how* you are thinking about your scenario.

The Sense of Infallible Thinking

But my logic seems so right. When I use my sense of reason, or common sense, I sometimes just don't see how I could be wrong.

I know what you mean. We tend to think of reason as an abstract tool that, if applied correctly, can always lead us to the right conclusions.

So when we try to make sense out of our experience, we think that as long as our reasoning is sound, our conclusions are too.

But reason doesn't work in a vacuum. Reason always consists of our assigning meaning to our experience, to incoming information, based on *what we think* we already know. Our common sensibility always presupposes that a certain story is true and uses this story to give new information meaning. The context for interpreting new information is then continually based upon the information that preceded it.

This is because we have a propensity for making sense of information as we receive it. Rather than take all the facts and see what story best ties them all together, we usually just try to tack on new info to our old stories. As each new piece of information comes in, we try to make sense out of it by making an assumption about how the pieces are "supposed to fit." Dr. de Bono illustrates this point with the following figure.[6]

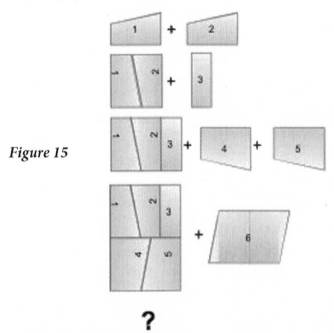

Figure 15

Just because all the data we've collected so far (all the things we've experienced up to a certain point) seem to fit together in a certain way, it doesn't make our assumptions correct. It doesn't necessarily make our underlying story true. In this case, the last piece, #6, does not seem to fit our assumptions. This is what happens when something doesn't make sense.

This illustrates that arriving information was used to simply reinforce our initial assumptions of what we thought was the big picture of how everything worked. The tendency was to try to "fit in" new data as it arrived rather than try to investigate whether or not there were alternative ways to organizing it all.

This idea also helps explain why some solutions seem obvious and logical in hindsight even though the answer was achieved through insight rather than deductive reasoning. Logic tries to fit things into pre-existing patterns, thereby reinforcing them. It is not meant to cut across into new patterns.

Are you saying logic is useless?

No. When assumptions change, logic has a new pattern to work with and can be used effectively to recognize the new relationships between data. Though logic may not have been used to find new assumptions, once the new assumptions are found, things can seem logical in hindsight.

Figure 16

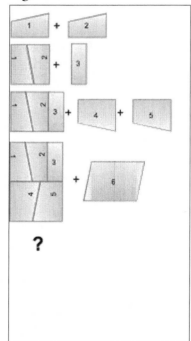 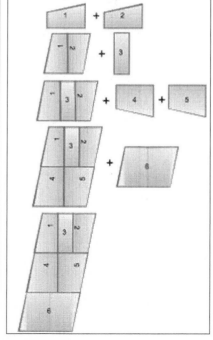

It is only by thinking differently that we could have attained the insight to change our initial assumption to a parallelogram pattern. We could not have found this through logic or reason, though they are very useful for verifying the usefulness of the new pattern and for implementing it to make sense out of new data as it comes in.

Tension and conflict can arise because of the value judgments we make based on information we interpret through *our own* assumed patterns rather than through the stories from which they originate. Think of all the assumptions we make about that look somebody gives us in the hallway, the conclusions we come to about people's behavior, or the judgments we make of other cultures because we see them in terms of our own paradigms rather than seeing them in their own native contexts.

Different ethnic groups, religious groups, social classes, or political parties may see each other as barbaric, unscientific, too scientific, vulgar, childish, ignorant, selfish, offensive, prudish, or immoral. But once they get to understand what somebody else's customs mean on their own terms, their perceptions could change.

Sometimes, bad means good and no means yes. Sometimes, the guy giving you the middle finger may just be saying that you're number one (though probably less frequently than I'd like). Or sometimes, the messengers of love and knowledge can be disregarded or even killed because they look unusual, say crazy things, or act in ways that are out of the ordinary. We can never give others a fair shake if we don't try looking at them through their own paradigm.

Fortunately, we always have the choice to perceive the world through the lens of a different context.

The assumptions we make about how to run a meeting, how to design a product, how to handle a crisis, how to paint, or how to make music can often cause us to get stuck or lead us down frustrating roads. Often we think getting new or better information will solve our dilemmas—better data, new research, or finding the right book (though I think the one you're holding in your hands is pretty useful). On the other hand, it could very well be that we have all the information we need, but we just don't have the right way to put it all together.

It could be that we need to alter the assumptions of what the information means to us. It could be that what we think about isn't the issue, but rather how we think about it is.

CHAPTER FIVE

The Stage of Innocence

In the previous two chapters, we explored the state of our mind at the beginning of the Creative Journey. That's the neurological story of our common sensibilities, its importance, and why it can be so hard to step out of the streams of our ingrained ideas and perceptions—hard to empty ourselves in order to make room for the creative spirit.

A Brief Summary of The Ordinary World

The neuroscience behind our more common thought processes reveals that we depend on pattern recognition and other mental short cuts to make sense of the world. In other words, even what appears to be pure reason is subjective based on our pre-existing neural structures, our prior experiences.

Short cut mechanisms, such as pattern recognition, are stress responses that keep us alive in threatening environments. Though useful for certain types of problem solving, when allowed to remain predominant, they limit our experience of the world and our access to fresh ideas, alternative perspectives, and new beliefs. These short cut mechanisms tend to reinforce pre-existing neural networks and firing patterns. In light of this, thinking differently can now be viewed as activating neural firing patterns that differ from our habitual ones.

Is this 'neuroscientific' perspective of the creative process more useful than the others we observed earlier from the top of the tower?

I do not claim that the perspective we have adopted here is more useful than others. However, it is based on an understanding of how our brain does its job. Also, this perspective has received the least attention in popular creativity discussions, though it is a very significant perspective. Our snap judgment tells us that the neuroscience perspective can be tedious, but it need not be so. Besides, it provides a very sound scientific base for the creative process—something the other perspectives lack.

Are quick judgments bad?

Not always. Instant decisions are necessary when we do not have time to consider alternatives. A good hunch can be very powerful and informative. But when we are trying to find creative ideas and solutions, quick decisions and judgments inherently limit us because they arise from our prior experiences or pre-existing neural structures. In other words, to find something new, we cannot really depend on the old.

It's critical to realize that all our important decisions need not be automatic—need not be without careful deliberation, so why not take the time to bring in various perspectives when we can, especially in situations where we find ourselves stuck after following a hunch.

Won't we appear indecisive and weak if we don't size up and resolve an issue quickly?

Is it better to appear decisive than be creative? A sense of humor about our perceptions and ourselves is what we need in situations where we feel attacked because somebody challenges our point of view. Some of us tend to take alternate views and opinions very personally and end up as strong defenders of our own ideas without realizing that our viewpoint could be one of many. Instead, we can see it as an opportunity to expose ourselves to other's ideas and opinions, which can present us with alternative perspectives and make us more creative.

Unfortunately, it's not always easy for us to change our assumptions. Look at how difficult it has been for some cultures to deal with gender and racial biases. Look at how strongly we can hold onto our beliefs without the willingness to explore other points of view.

It sounds like you're advocating that we shouldn't have strong beliefs.

It's wonderful to have strong beliefs. They help us make sense of an ever-changing world. They ground us and help stabilize our experiences. They make our decision making process simple and manageable. They provide an anchor when we can easily be drifted off by the erratic winds out to the abyss of the sea.

This is why living on our very own island of pickles and doughnuts is important before beginning our Creative Journey. Set assumptions and automatic perceptions are very often the first stage of the creative process.

It is here where we work hard to become skilled and gain knowledge. It is that stage of the creative process where Mozart spent hours practicing the piano and learning music theory and where the Kellogg brothers became experts on grain. At this stage, we learn the craft of sculpting, or learn the basics of running a business, or do the groundwork for numerous other endeavors.

In the words of neuroscience, this is the stage when we form neural structures (assumptions and automatic perceptions) associated with our endeavor. Here, we prepare ourselves to be receptive to creative insight (Pasteur's experiments before the lucky accident) and prepare ourselves for being able to turn these insights into some sort of meaningful reality—either as an artistic expression, a product, a business, a solution to a problem, an invention, a new way of living our lives etc...

Moving Beyond the Ordinary World

In my own Creative Journey, I spent several years of my life practicing music, developing my creative writing skills, and sweating nervously in front of fellow students doing improvisational activities. And within the last couple of years, my head was often buried in books. I would spend long hours in the library, bookstore, or coffee shop learning as much as I could about creative thinking and the creative process.

Writing a book wasn't easy for me. It took a lot of effort and preparation before I ever wrote my first sentence. In fact, during this preparation stage, the idea of actually writing a book seemed like an impossibility—a task reserved for "real writers."

"I was an engineer," I kept telling myself. "Not a writer."

In order to move beyond this stage, in order to get ourselves unstuck and overcome our creative blocks, we must first realize that alternatives exist regardless of how convinced we are that they don't. This is the major obstacle associated with this stage of the creative process, which is why I emphasized this point in Chapter 1.

The first task of the creative hero is then to form perceptions while realizing that perceptions are inherently limited. We must realize that our island is only one amongst many floating in a vast sea of possibilities.

Summary:

- 1st Stage: The Ordinary World
- Archetype: The Innocent
- Task: To Acknowledge an Imperfect World View
- Obstacle: Complacency

The 2nd Aspect

Answering the Call to Think Differently

The Beginning of the Beggar's Tale

The beggar sat up, dusted off his leather pants, and put on his coat that he had been using as a pillow. He leaned against the tree, sighed, and began speaking.

"Sit and I will tell you the story of how I pursued this treasure. I will tell you the story of how I pursued it so that you may know the terrain and discover it yourself. "

The villagers looked at each other, as if waiting for another to be the first to take action.

"But I don't want to sit here," the farmer said hesitantly. "The grass is wet and I wouldn't want to dirty my loins."

The villagers all bobbed their heads and mumbled in agreement, although what they were truly afraid of was learning what existed beyond the shore. They were afraid of the prospect of leaving the island.

"If you do not want to live a life of pickles and doughnuts forever, I suggest you sit and listen. Otherwise, you'll be like everyone else who has ever entered the carnival—leaving with a burning flame of enthusiasm, only to have their motivation dwindle to a tiny flickering spark by the time they reach their pickle hut. As soon as you leave here, your experience of the carnival will be but a distant memory."

The men looked at each other and began grumbling some more.

Then, suddenly, one of the villagers dropped to the grass. And seeing this, the others quickly followed.

As soon as they all sat down, the tone of the conversation changed from one of pessimism to one of hope. "The winter wreaked such havoc on our village… There must be something different we can do to recover… There must be new ideas that we can implement… There must be more to this island than pickles and doughnuts."

They all became so involved in their inner dialogues that they failed to notice it was the village drunk that initially fell to the ground out of pure loss of equilibrium. But they all did sit on the ground just the same.

"You see, at the other end of the island, there is a bridge over a dangerous pit that you must walk across."

"A pit?" they asked with trepidation.

"Yes. But fear not, because the bridge is safe. Once you cross over the pit, you will find a boat docked on the shore."

"A boat?" They all gasped at the thought.

"Those aren't real," remarked the religious person.

"I thought those were only in fairy tales," added the chef.

"I know," replied the beggar. "But they really do exist. And you must use it to travel west. West is the direction the sun travels, so that is the direction you too must travel."

The doughnut maker remained fearful. "But from what I've heard, boats aren't safe! The stories always tell tales of how they could capsize, get lost at sea, get caught in a storm…."

"Yes. That is all true. That is why you must have hope. All adventures worth having require it. You must have hope that there is something worth pursuing outside of the island."

CHAPTER SIX
Crossing the Threshold:
Should I Stay or Should I Go?

Going to dinner with my friends is often a frustrating experience. It can sound like a great idea at first. But deciding on where to go can be such a pain.

The typical scene usually comes in two shades.

The first: Everyone gathers at somebody's house, we stare at each other waiting for somebody to make a decision on where to go, and every suggestion somebody makes is immediately shot down by another.

How about we go to Café Jay's?
>   - I think it's too expensive.
How about Jay's Burger Joint?
>   - I think it's too greasy.
How about The Bistro on Jay Street?
>   - I think it's too far. Plus, I just ate there yesterday.

The second: Everyone gathers at somebody's house, we stare at each other waiting for somebody to make a decision on where to go, but there are just so many darn options that nobody knows what to do. As a result, we spend more than half the night trapped in the hallway of somebody's house instead of enjoying ourselves at the restaurant.

Being aware that alternatives may exist just makes you more aware of the depths of possibilities. It allows you to take the first step in the creative process. But it does not necessarily motivate you to actually jump into it. We can often be stuck battling negative thoughts or simply be mesmerized by all the directions we can go.

Rather than wait in the hallway of whatever creative endeavor you've chosen to pursue, you may just have more fun crossing that threshold and trying out Jay's Burger Joint. One greasy burger ain't gonna kill you.

...at least not immediately.

Trapped in Thought: Stuck on a Seesaw with Bert and Ernie

I often get stuck thinking about alternatives. Why is that?

We can get caught up in always thinking that the grass is greener on the other side of the fence. We can become so preoccupied thinking and dreaming about the next best thing that we never get around to actually exploring alternatives. It's as if we fall so in love with just the idea of creating a new painting that we never get around to touching the canvas.

On the flip side, we can get caught up in our pessimistic thoughts. We can find ourselves playing mental loops that tell us that there are no other possibilities: *There is no other way to write this song, or design this product, or solve this crisis. There is no other course of action worth investigating.* Often it seems like we are trying to convince ourselves that it's all been done before, that we've already tried everything.

Both of these feelings are the result of our habitual thought patterns in action. Just like our snap judgment (short cut) mechanisms discussed earlier, they are based on another mental rule of thumb and have their roots in trying to keep us safe.

Try imagining yourself on a seesaw. Internally, your unconscious is doing its best to keep you balanced. If you are focused, busy contently doing whatever you are doing, it's as if you're sitting by yourselves on the seesaw, completely tipped over to one side. In order to balance things out, your unconscious may send over a little playmate, Ernie, to sit with you on the other end of the seesaw. In this case, Ernie would be that little voice that tells you that alternatives exist. He'd be the voice telling you how lovely it would be to try something new. *Try this. Try that. There's so much more you can do than what you're doing.*

As some of you have noticed, Ernie can be a little talkative.

On the other hand, if all you are doing is thinking about alternatives, your unconscious may send over Bert to remind you how dangerous it may be to deviate from where you are. Bert is the voice that reminds you of the inherent hazards of venturing into uncharted waters. *Don't do this. Don't try that. There's nothing more you can do than what you're doing. And even if there were, it wouldn't be worth it.*

Bert too can be chatty, not to mention very convincing.

So whenever you stray to one side of the seesaw, thoughts may enter your conscious mind in an attempt to keep you balanced.

The problem is that we can fall prey to the habitual thoughts of these two states. We become easily convinced to follow either Bert or Ernie. We can get addicted to the high-energy optimism that accompanies thinking about new alternatives. This can prevent us from choosing any alternative and taking it further. Or, if addicted to the gravity of Bert's pessimism, the world can simply seem to be closed and limiting.

So how do we deal with Bert and Ernie?

The creative process includes both of these habitual thought patterns, but knowing that they are naturally part of the creative process—a survival response of our mind—will make us less prone to being caught up in either pattern of thought.

I know Bert and Ernie can be very annoying. When we simply want to focus on our task, Ernie shows up wanting us to go out and play. When we want to step out the door, Bert tries to convince us that it'll be no fun to leave the house. As a result, we can develop the overwhelming urge to just give Bert and Ernie a good spanking. And often we do just that—we fight our thoughts. But slapping them around simply wastes our energy and is time spent not participating in the creative process.

When either Bert or Ernie shows up, we simply need to wave hi and acknowledge their presence. If we ignore them, we may soon find ourselves blindly stuck on one side of the seesaw—stuck either in eternal pessimism or eternal optimism without any eye toward reality. The same is true if we clutch onto one or the other for dear life. On the other hand, if we fight them, we waste our precious time and energy.

The easiest way to handle Bert and Ernie is to thank them for joining us. This allows us to be more conscious of the context of our thoughts and actions giving us control over them instead of seesawing at their mercy.

Overcoming Negative Thoughts: Finding Context

Imagine being in a meeting. You may have some very intelligent people who can all agree that there are alternative ways of doing things, yet they refuse to pursue them. It may be that they are resistant because they think it would be a waste of time and energy.

Similarly, in our individual circumstances, we can be aware that alternative paths and perceptions are possible, but we are convinced by

Bert and feel that exploring options would not be a worthwhile pursuit.

What creative endeavor comes without some form of risk—failure, embarrassment, loss of time and effort, being "wrong?" Ask any successful investor, inventor, or artist, and you'll hear a story of risk-taking.

How do I overcome my negative thoughts?

Though new paths may seem dangerous because they are unfamiliar, they are usually not as life threatening as we make them out to be. Exploring the possibility of a new music form or a new way to make a living may feel dangerous, but it certainly won't put you in immediately life-threatening situations. It's not as if music critics will literally charge you like a tiger or your mortgage lender will jump out of the trees piercing your neck with a blow dart like some African pygmy bushman.

The fact is that we may be placing ourselves in even greater danger by *not* looking for creative solutions.

To successfully participate in the creative process, we must realize that we often tend to exaggerate the magnitude or significance of failure. This is another habitual pattern of thought. Instead, you can choose how you think of failure: be afraid of it or give it context by seeing it as part of the learning process—as another natural part of the creative process.

In writing this book, I would sometimes catch myself thinking that my efforts were worthless, that they wouldn't amount to anything. There would be seconds, minutes, sometimes days when it felt that all this effort spent trying to create something new was a waste of time and that my energies could be better used in other things. This may or may not be true, but I would never find out until I finished.

Just realizing that this pessimism was a natural part of the process made it much easier for me to move on. It gave this element of the process—my experience of self-doubt—context and, thereby, meaning. It was no more just "negative" thoughts.

I chose to put my experience of pessimism within a story of a hopeful process rather than a hopeless one, and you hold the result in your hands.

The Time for Alternatives

Wouldn't it be a pain to always think about alternatives? I'd never get anything done.

Thinking incessantly about alternatives can lead to an analysis paralysis. You probably had an infinite number of decisions to make just within the last 24 hours: what clothes to wear, what to eat, what book to read, how to sit on your chair, what room to do your reading in. Every action you made was inherently laden with several possibilities.

Often, it really isn't necessary, or worthwhile, to pursue alternatives. Sometimes, our energy really is better off focused on other tasks. You could have spent the entire day thinking about all the possible ways to read this book: on your bed, on the floor, in your kitchen, at the coffee shop, in the library, at the bookstore, in your car while driving, in the shower because you want to be "different." Valuable time would have been wasted when you could have used it instead to pursue the more important task of actually reading the book.

However, what happens when we are faced with larger issues or more critical decisions? If we continue to act and react the way we have always done, we cannot expect anything to change. We will never learn, improve, or create anything unique. We would never manifest new works of art, unique technologies, or creative solutions.

So the idea isn't that we need to pursue alternatives all the time. The idea is that when we want to think differently, when we want to pursue a creative endeavor, we must be willing to accept that alternatives are worthwhile to pursue.

The point is that it may be in our best interest to frequently stop and re-evaluate how we do things and how we perceive the world we live in.

CHAPTER SEVEN
The Stage of Becoming an Orphan

We are innocent in the first stage, unaware of alternatives, thinking we have no choices of perception or behavior. But now, in this second stage, we have accepted that there may be alternative ways of thinking and acting. Our conscious mind starts to question its preconceptions—the dominant neural networks that help us make snap judgments and decisions. In this stage, we are *called* to explore other possibilities. In this stage, we confront the decision to either stay on our island or see what exists beyond it.

Answering the Call

This call can take on many forms—the urge to do something new, to work on debt or health issues, or to maintain a competitive edge to name a few. In this sense, every moment of every life is a call. It is a continuous call to choose to do things differently.

Choosing to approach a problem differently or choosing to respond to one's environment differently is often difficult. We are unwilling to put in the effort not only because of complacency, but also because it means letting go of firmly rooted ways and ideas. These things are what often define our internal world, and letting them go is akin to losing our home. In many ways, we can feel like orphans in this stage because it is here that we face the prospect of leaving our ordinary world behind.

It is also here that we realize that by pursuing a creative endeavor, we may have to leave some people behind, if only temporarily, because the ordinary world is where most people reside. People might make fun of us, or give us dirty looks, or talk about how odd we are behind our backs. But remember, they are basing their judgments on their assumptions and beliefs that we are challenging. Martin Luther King had his fair share of detractors. Galileo was condemned for believing in Copernicus's sun-centered cosmology.

There also may be some in the family who think that Uncle Charlie was a nut for believing that Smurfs lived under his bed.

> Answering the call to be creative doesn't mean you'll be right. It just means you have given yourself the opportunity to discover something new.

Jazz pianist Dave Brubeck was heeding the call when he decided to explore Middle Eastern and Indian music. Before his exploration, his compositions (along with the majority of jazz tunes) were written in a 4/4-meter. After his exploration, he was inspired to compose one of his most famous songs, *Take Five*, which is exclusively in 5/4 meter, and a new jazz standard was born. It is also in this second stage that we realize there may be a non-linear way to approach a problem that requires lateral thinking.

Crossing the Threshold

In essence, this is the stage where we must turn our back on the light of the familiar to face the darkness of the unknown. Jazz musician and composer Benny Golson echoes these sentiments below:

> The creative person always walks two steps into the darkness. Everybody can see what's in the light. They can imitate it, they can underscore it, they can modify it, and they can reshape it. But the real heroes delve in darkness of the unknown. It's where you discover 'other things'. I say other things because when the new things are discovered, they have no name....[1]

Between the light of the ordinary world and the dark, ambiguous world of possibility is a pit we must cross—the Pit of Pessimism. The chef may resist changing a recipe because she lacks the optimism to believe in a new dish. The artist may continue painting in the same style because she fears alienating her admirers. The author may feel obliged to write in the same genre because she has doubts that she can appeal to a new audience. In solving life's many problems, some may be cynical of new approaches, afraid of failing, wasting time, or looking foolish trying something unusual.

According to Seymour Epstein, psychologist at the University of Massachusetts, many academically smart individuals are unable to be creative. Epstein found that many of these people "hold back from new challenges because they lack the necessary emotional smarts."[2] The creative hero must be curious to find out if what she fears is simply "false evidence assumed real." It is therefore our task at this stage to let go of the need to be "right" in order to find hope in exploring new endeavors. Only by crossing the Pit of Pessimism with the aid of creative curiosity can we reach our new home in the Sea of Possibilities.

Finding Hope

There are several ways you can find hope in your endeavors.

- First, you can find hope by looking at the example of others. You can see others who have participated in the creative process and gain assurance that it is possible to find alternatives. This doesn't just mean looking at famous people. This could also mean looking at your neighbor, a coworker, a classmate, a relative, or a friend. It could mean looking at other successful communities, organizations, or corporations. You may want to put yourself in an environment with others who are also going through the creative process, whether it is in a class, a workshop, or a club. Heck, you can even start your own group.

- Another way to find hope is by reflecting on past experience. If you're looking to be creative in how you do business or in your approach to your career path, you may want to reflect on other endeavors where you were successfully creative. You can reflect on the time you successfully concocted a new dish, or put together a new clothing ensemble, or even wrote a letter. We've all already gone through the creative process to some degree somewhere along the way.

- You can also decide to try being creative in a field you feel more comfortable in at first or one that seems less daunting.

It could be painting, or creative writing, or playing any number of creativity games, board games, or participating in any improvisational activity. The point isn't necessarily to be successful, or to win, but to learn what the process feels like so that you can lessen your fear by gaining familiarity. This way you can have more hope in the fruitfulness of the process itself.

You can imagine then how important hope is in groups wishing to participate in a creative endeavor. If some of those involved do not have hope that their efforts may be fruitful, they may inhibit the creative process—unconsciously sabotaging the creative efforts of the group.

In order for a group to undertake the creative process, it is best that all participants accept that what they are doing is worthwhile. You can lay it out as a ground rule, but coerced beliefs hardly ever stick. Instead, it may be better to provide examples, have them reflect on past experience, or have them participate in exercises that make them more aware of the efficacy of the process.

Lastly, hope often arises out of necessity. Sometimes, when strong winds cross our path, we have no choice but be pushed across the Pit of Pessimism. Sometimes, stormy winters turn our worlds upside down, leaving us with nothing else to hold onto but hope.

Summary:
- 2nd Stage: The Call and Crossing the Threshold
- Archetype: The Orphan
- Task: Having Hope in the Creative Journey
- Obstacle: The Pit of Pessimism

The 3rd Aspect
Entering the Sea of Possibilities

The Fire Breathing Dragon

The beggar stood up and removed his jacket. He then began to run around the men, chasing the evening breeze, holding his jacket as if it were some sort of kite.

"It was a wonderful feeling being at sea and heading west. It was freeing. The cool sea winds dashing across my face, as the sunlight kept me warm. My first day at sea was an exhilarating experience."

"What did you take with you on your adventure?" asked the laborer.

"Well, lots of stuff…lots of pickles and doughnuts of course."

"Of course!" the villagers all replied.

"As the sun began to set on my first day at sea, it became dark, and being alone at sea in the dark was very frightening. The island was all I had ever known, and to be away from it was deathly terrifying."

"How did you cope with that?" asked the doughnut maker.

"It was difficult. But what made it worse was that on that night, my very first night, I was awakened by the flames of a dragon."

The men gasped.

"Dragon?" the religious person blurted out. "I thought those were only in bedtime stories?"

"Yes, I know. They're real though. Believe me. When you have one breathing flames that scorch the hairs off your neck, you'll know for yourself. You needn't believe me now."

The chef was enthralled. "So what did you do?"

"Nothing."

"Nothing?"

"Nothing…what was I supposed to do? Take off all my clothes

and run around naked like a mad man?"

"Your naked body scaring off a fire-breathing dragon?" replied the farmer. "That's something I could definitely believe."

The beggar squinted his eyes with contempt. "The point is I couldn't think of anything to do. Nothing. I had no thoughts. My mind was empty of them. Being scared can do one of two things—fill your head or empty it completely. It was in those empty moments that I realized that the beast had no interest in me. It wasn't my odor that attracted him. It was the smell of my pickles and doughnuts."

The men let out a groan.

"So I threw them as far as I could—threw them into the sea. The dragon chased after them, and let me be, without any harm done."

The villagers stared at the beggar in astonishment and disbelief.

"And it was then, for the first time in my life, that I was truly alone…without even one pickle or one doughnut."

CHAPTER EIGHT
Examining the Origins of Our Dominant Ideas and Behaviors

There can be a certain thrill associated with entering into the creative process. Just as with any new endeavor, mustering up the courage to try something different may result in heightened excitement. But though we set sail and take a few steps outside our familiar surroundings, we often find a way to take our old ways with us.

Letting go of our old habits and perceptions can be daunting. Often, they have worked well in the past, and letting them go can feel as if we are jumping off of a trapeze without a net...or like running out into the street naked.*   To compensate, we may vigorously defend our old methods and conceptions, convince ourselves that we have some sort of magical writer's block, or simply refuse to jump into the unknown for a number of insincere reasons.

It's great to have strong ideas, opinions, and beliefs. But in order to grow, learn, improve, or create something unique, we will have to turn our assumptions on their heads. We must step out of the stream of our firmly ingrained beliefs, paradigms, and perceptions.

- Dean Ornish ventured away from old, firmly ingrained beliefs and discovered that heart disease could be treated through diet, exercise, and meditation. At one point, a leading cardiologist asked Dr. Ornish why he wanted to try something so 'radical' as lifestyle changes rather than 'something more conventional,' such as bypass surgery.

---

*But I'm too ugly to run into the street without clothes! I'll just die from embarrassment! —Most likely not true. I can't believe anybody reading this book isn't exceptionally pleasing on the eyes—metaphorically speaking.

- Thomas Edison even hired research assistants based on their ability to have an open mind. Edison would invite candidates to have a bowl of soup. If they seasoned it before tasting it, he refused to hire them because they had built in assumptions about the soup without trying it.
- It was because of firmly rooted beliefs that in 1927, Harry Warner, former president of Warner Brothers, once asked, "Who the hell wants to hear actors talk?"

What if I don't want to leave my worldview behind forever?

We mustn't forget that we are only *temporarily* leaving our dominant beliefs. It is only done for this particular phase of the creative process. It is done so that we can free ourselves to explore alternatives. We need not leave an idea behind forever. We can always return to our old garments in case it gets too chilly.

> If you truly believe your old ideas are valid and your old patterns of behavior are optimal, then they will always be there for you when you return.

When we are done investigating alternatives, we are then free to once again return to our old ideas and perceptions. However, I doubt anyone at Warner Brothers continues to believe that films should all still be silent. Though I guess that may depend on who is acting in them.

Origins of Our Dominant Perceptions

Where do our ingrained ideas and behaviors come from?

There is this great anecdote about a pygmy (a real one, not a fictitious one masquerading as a debt collector).[1] For the first time in his life, he was taken on a ride on a motorized vehicle and ventured from his home in the dense forest out into the open plains. Soon on his ride, he noticed insects hovering about in front of him. As he and his driver continued onward, the pygmy watched in amazement as the insects began to slowly grow to enormous sizes as he approached them.

"What kind of magical insects are these?" he asked, dumbfounded.

"Those aren't insects," replied his driver. "We are just getting closer and closer to buffalo."

Though I wasn't there with the two men on their drive, I could imagine how shaken the pygmy must have been to have his perceptions misled by his dominant worldview—one that was based upon living in the midst of a dense jungle and not on a speeding motor vehicle on a vast plain.

In general, our neural networks can be seen as the biological container of our worldviews. They are tied to the different stories we use to make sense of what is around us. Our neural structures are like a web of meaning that help form the conceptual space of our perceptions—what we feel is possible—and provide boundaries and rules that shape our interaction with the world. Think back to your perception of possibilities when trying to solve the puzzle of the man who died at the age of 27 or the two men who died in the woods.

These neural structures originate from a combination of genetic inheritance and life experiences. By taking a closer look at the origins of these neural structures, we may start to understand why we feel so emotionally tied to the world-view and belief systems they correspond to.

Hard-wired By Genetics

Our DNA determines many of our neural networks. For example, there are many regions in our neocortex that have been pre-wired for vision, hearing, touch, and motor functions. Also, we are pre-wired for many basic emotional responses and for particularly human ways of perceiving the world. It's as if just enough basic, fundamental tasks were assigned to a small population of our mental metropolis in order to start running the city before we were even born (cook, cleaner, financier)—assigned by our parents' DNA, their parents before them etc.

Developed and Learned

All of the neural networks not pre-wired by our genes are learned as we live our lives. In other words, though some people in our mental metropolis were assigned to be cooks in the city, specifics such as how to cook, what to cook, where to cook, and who to feed, may be determined through our lived experience in the world.

- The formation of learned neural networks appears to begin

117

very early in human development. There is even evidence that our neural networks are actively learning prior to birth. For example, infants are able to distinguish the mother's voice from other voices within the first 2-3 days after birth because they are exposed to it while in the womb.[2] The malleability of neural structures is what allows children to learn languages, speech, and motor coordination.

- Our physical environment greatly affects our neural structures. For example, the pygmy in our earlier anecdote was unaccustomed to seeing beyond a few feet in front of him because he lived exclusively within dense forests. His capacities of perception were ill equipped to handle a situation where he needed to see far.

And in general, all the cultures that we grow up in, and are exposed to, can affect our paradigms. All types of groups—from Western to Eastern societies, from physicists to philosophers, from armed forces to athletes—will hold certain assumptions about reality and what is possible, acceptable, and valued.

A musician's world may revolve around their instrument, their music, and their upcoming gigs. A good day may revolve around the quality of their performance or in a completed composition. A long distance runner's world may be very different. It may revolve around their shoes, their running trail, and their upcoming race. A stack of pancakes after an arduous run could be enough to make their day—at least it does mine.

These paradigms are stored and passed along through various cultural devices and traditions. Examples of these devices include the stories we tell one another through film, television, songs, formal education, informal education, and all other media. We participate in cultural traditions, such as birthday celebrations, funerals, wedding ceremonies, and watching *Monday Night Football*, just to name a few. A quick reflection on the activities that shape our lives can reveal many more. They also reveal the underlying narratives that we unconsciously use to guide our lives.

Our friends, family, coworkers, classmates, teachers, and the world at large continually influence our perceptions and paradigms. By sharing similar worldviews, we can more easily communicate with one another since we have shared meaning. We can appreciate the same jokes. We can become closer communities because these shared paradigms provide us with common bonds. For instance, runners can appreciate the experience of running a marathon in a way a non-runner can't. The same is true for the artist, businessperson, parent, and any other segment of society.

And through these paradigms, we are able to learn from the shared experiences of others.

But as we've already discussed, when we hold onto these paradigms too tightly, we may become blind to the value of other worldviews and the possibility of other perceptions, solutions, and ideas. Heart disease would only be treated with surgery and films would have always been silent if nobody had the courage to let go of established paradigms.

Reflect upon your current creative endeavor or the one you're thinking of pursuing. What are the assumptions you are making about how you will do it, what you need in order to do it, what success would look like etc…? What may be the underlying assumptions preventing you from moving on? Are you aware of where these assumptions come from? Realizing this may be your first step towards altering them.

Resistance to Change

Why is it hard to alter our perceptions and paradigms?

Emotional Reactions

One reason our perceptions and thoughts can seem so fixed is that they can be heavily influenced by our emotions.

Think back to when you were younger. Do you remember ever being in a darkened room, scared of the sound of every creek, movement of the drapes, or whisper of the wind? One moment, you're in the safe confines of your bedroom. In the next, your fears are triggered by these harmless sounds and sights. And before you know it, you're convinced that there is a three hundred pound invisible monster lurking in your closet that nobody in the house has ever seen.

This type of scenario still happens to us in our adulthood. Maybe, even the exact same scenario.

Our emotional reactions to circumstances and scenarios can quickly trigger a particular perception or interpretation of what we are experiencing. We see a blank canvas, then become frustrated, and before we know it, we perceive our process as hopeless. We hear somebody speaking in a different language, become angered, and then suddenly, we are convinced that we are in the midst of terrorists. Or we see somebody who is dressed a certain way, then become fearful, and without any other supporting information, we perceive ourselves to be in a dangerous situation with a hoodlum.

Out of habit, we may then start fantasizing and assigning exaggerated meaning to our experience. We contextualize our emotions with assumed stories that further fuel our emotions that further enlarge our stories. As a result, our perceptions can "lock in" because we feed into our emotional reactions, regardless of how accurate or appropriate they are to the circumstance.

"Damn, I'm never going to get anything interesting on this canvas. I'm a terrible artist...."

"Hey, those people are speaking that foreign gibberish. They're going to steal all our jobs or try to take over this plane!"

"Oh, no! He might have a gun or a knife. He might be a gang member who assaulted his teacher when he was 12 and now walks the streets as a thug, stalking unsuspecting authors of books on creativity."

The emotional response can trigger an intellectual one that further perpetuates our emotions. In the blink of an eye a quirky gesture from a politician can be misconstrued by her opposing party as a sign of ignorance, weakness, disrespect, aggression, or any number of assumed meanings. Without a second's notice, she is labeled as a fascist, socialist, communist, racist, narcissist, hedonist, plagiarist, contortionist, and any other word ending in "ist."

...all because she was caught simply scratching her itchy nose or shooing away a mosquito.

How do we deal with our emotional reactions?

Again, these emotional responses are simply our unconscious trying to help us maintain balance, just as it does through our thoughtful playmates Bert and Ernie. They are another rule of thumb, one that gives us enough energy to run at the sight of a tiger or to fight when we are attacked. However, too often these energies are triggered by less than immediate threats. And more often than not in the modern age, these energies are triggered by circumstances that pose no mortal threat at all—a writer's blank computer screen, criticism from a peer, a failed product idea, or a simple gesture from a stranger.

The remedy is the same. Rather than blindly follow our emotions down into the rabbit hole of exaggerated perceptions, we need to develop a more conscious relationship to them. We need to acknowledge them, see what they may be indicating (life-threatening danger or overreaction to our circumstances), and make a more conscious decision on how to respond to them.

We already know that we have a propensity for misperception and overgeneralization, so why not take a deep breath and put our circumstance in perspective. That blank canvas may in fact be your masterpiece in waiting and not an indicator that you should quit painting.

Weren't all masterpieces blank at their start?

So, our emotions affect our perception, our perception in turn aggravates our emotional response, and the vicious cycle goes on until we accept the emotion and consciously explain it away—it's the fear of darkness that created the monster lurking in our closet. Apart from our emotions, there also seems to be a biological reason why we dislike change or things different.

Reinforcing Our Old Ideas: Hebbian Learning

As we have seen, neural connectivity can be strengthened through repetition. The more we are exposed to our spouse, the stronger the association is between our spouse and her/his characteristics (tall, dark haired, pudgy, distinctive odor etc.) These characteristics can become so tied to our notion of our spouse that other objects with similar traits (such as that random stranger at the grocery store who looked like a dead ringer from behind) can accidentally place us in some very uncomfortable hugging situations. Though for the most part, we have no difficulty distinguishing our spouse from the grocery clerk when we take a closer look.

How does Hebbian Learning work?

The strengthening of these associations is explained by a theory proposed by psychologist Donald Hebb. The more often a group of neurons are activated at about the same time, the more efficient the signaling between them becomes, like greasing the connecting pipes in order to make them work better. As a result, their connectivity becomes "stronger."

For example, when we are exposed to a glass of wine, neurons are activated by the way the wine smells, tastes, looks, feels etc. The more we are exposed to the same type of wine, the stronger the neural connection between the neurons associated with each of these attributes. This is why some wine aficionados can differentiate between a 2005 South African Bored Doe and a 1985 Marilyn Merlot. It is also why we are adept at distinguishing our child Milli from the neighbor's child Vanilli. Though we may be fooled by their similarities in a quick glance, we know who's who upon closer inspection.

This theory helps explain the relative staying power of general and procedural memories as compared to those that are more specific and declarative in nature. For instance, exposure to specific birds, such as a Blue Jay or a Fluffy-backed Tit Babbler,* will each activate particular neural networks. Conversely, because both are birds, neural networks associated with the broad concept of a bird will be activated both times. Our general concept of what a "bird" is gains double strength.

Hebbian learning then has great implications for our perception and world-views. Because it is our nature to make sense of the world by trying to fit new information into our old stories, we end up just firming up our old stories. Any new *specific* experience we have will tend to simply reinforce our *general* paradigm. If our dominant paradigm is the belief that being an entrepreneur is foolhardy, then we'll tend to see our lack of ideas and lack of progress as proof of that, further strengthening that story. On the other hand, if our dominant paradigm is the belief that entrepreneurship is the yellow brick road to happiness, then we may tend to see lack of ideas and progress as proof that we're on our way to success.

Because we habitually recognize patterns, we will likely organize the world into the same dominant patterns regardless of their authenticity or level of usability. We can see this with political pundits who can interpret just about anything as proof of their own point of view. Who knows what the more accurate perspectives are, but you'll never find out if you're stuck on one in particular.

---

* I didn't believe this was a real bird either when I first heard of it.

Drive toward Homeostasis

Why are we sometimes uncomfortable with the unfamiliar?

For the most part, we try to match the stories we tell ourselves of the world with the world itself. That way we know what to expect from our environment—what the dangers are, where the food is etc....We also have a drive to maintain homeostasis, which simply means we want to keep our relationship to our environment stable. Once Caveman Fred knew where saber tooth tigers were sleeping and where he could find good steak, he was set, and any change to these things was a threat to his survival. But as a result of our drive for homeostasis, it seems we have grown to favor the familiar and find displeasure in the unfamiliar.

- In one study, test subjects were shown a series of photographs of people's faces. When asked which face they like more, the subjects always favored the faces that were shown more often, regardless of the specific face. A similar experiment was done with musical melodies with comparable results.[3]

- In another experiment, subjects were shown pictures of unusual shapes for only 1msec at a time. This meant that the subjects were receiving data beneath conscious awareness, since 1msec is much too fast to consciously recognize or memorize the images they saw. The experimenters then paired each of these shapes with another that the subjects had not yet seen and showed the pair slowly to the subjects. Again, the subjects favored the pair that included the image they had seen more often.[4] These results seem to imply that the effects of familiarity on preference occur even if a person is not consciously aware of their stimuli—that we can be influenced subconsciously.

It appears then that there is a neurological basis for the tensions that can arise when people of different backgrounds and points of view interact. In our drive for survival, it seems that we strive to find stability between our environment and ourselves. When that balance is offset through exposure to different beliefs, customs, traditions, or by a change in our physical environment, we can feel uncomfortable or threatened. This is at the root of our biases and prejudices.

This also helps provide an explanation for why it can be so hard to deviate from the norm. It is difficult to be creative when part of our biology dictates we stick to what we know. If we are used to a particular process, method, approach to problems, or standards for success, we can feel uneasy about new ones. The same is true of all our ideas and behaviors.

When our external world no longer matches our internal one, we can have a biological reaction that requires us to either change our environment or change our internal structures—our stories of the *way things are* and the *way things are supposed to be done*.

But it's hard to think differently when we may have a biological propensity to stick with the familiar.

No wonder it can be so hard for Old Uncle Max to change his opinion, change his lifestyle, or to remember to put the toilet seat back down after use.

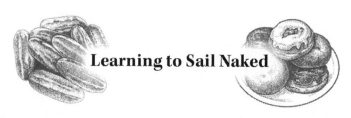

Learning to Sail Naked

he villagers couldn't imagine venturing out to sea without any pickles and doughnuts.

"I couldn't do that."

"Me neither."

"It's just not in me."

"If I were to throw out all my pickles and doughnuts, I might as well sail on a leaky ship."

The beggar nodded his head, acknowledging the villagers' concerns. "I know it seems that way, but we were born to do it. We all are. Even I did it. Plus, it wasn't as if I'd never have another pickle and doughnut again. As long as I made it back home, I knew I could have as many of them as I wanted. They were just waiting for me to return to the island."

The villagers sat in silence.

"Look, how many of you thought I was a dirty, old, drunk beggar when we first met?"

The villagers all raised their hands.

"And now that some time has passed, and you've gotten to know me a little better, how many of you still think I'm a dirty, old, drunk beggar?"

They all once again raised their hands.

"Oh...well, how many of you think I'm less of a drunk?"

"Oh, yes. Definitely less of a drunk than I thought," said the chef.

"Yes, you speak in complete sentences. So I must concur," added the farmer.

"See...you all *can* change your perceptions." The beggar then watched as the village drunk placed his index finger in his ear while sucking the thumb of the same hand.

"I still think you're a lush," replied the village drunk.

The beggar laughed and continued, "As unlikely as it may seem, even he can learn to think differently."

CHAPTER NINE
Scientific Evidence for the Possibility of Thinking Differently

I know too many people who are stuck in their beliefs, stuck to their old ways of doing things. Is there proof that we can make significant change to our thinking patterns?

Our beliefs and perceptions, our dominant neural networks, provide an anchor when we can easily be driven by the erratic winds and drift off to sea. But only by lifting the anchor can we hope to explore the rich breadth of the ocean.

Fortunately, though we have a neurological urge to dislike change, neuroscience also tells us that our brain has the ability to rewire itself. We can form new neural networks (an ability which is called neuroplasticity). What is more, our right and left hemispheres are so organized as to learn and come up with novel ideas.

The Story of Neuroplasticity

At the University of Wisconsin-Madison, Paul Bach-y-Rita has done the miraculous. He has given the sense of sight to the blind.[1]

Well sort of.

At the departments of rehabilitation medicine and biomedical engineering, a mechanism has been developed that allows a blind person to see through the sense of touch. They are able to gain spatial awareness that includes both perspective and depth through the use of this specialized mechanism. It has a camera used to capture visual information commonly associated with the eye and translates the images captured into tactile information that can be sensed through the skin of a hand or through the tongue.

Though the user may not experience the sense of sight in the same way others do, this finding is miraculous nonetheless. Remember, the third layer of our brain known as the neocortex, or new brain, is comprised of different lobes that are thought to specialize in different functions (processing sight, sound, touch etc…). What the researchers at the University of Wisconsin-Madison have shown is that these specialized lobes can be rewired to process other types of information. The brain is able to re-wire itself and adapt to change. In this case, the areas of the brain that specialized in dealing with information from touch actually changed to also deal with spatial awareness.*

Referring back to our mental metropolis, it's as if the folks at the financial district have also learned how to run a restaurant. At least now, if they ever lose their jobs because of a neurological market collapse, they can be useful at the next potluck.

A slightly less dramatic but equally relevant example is that of Japanese speakers. Japanese adults have difficulty discriminating between "R" and "L" sounds, such as in "rip" and "lip" because the Japanese language does not include the sound of the letter "L." Studies demonstrate that though Japanese infants are not born with this difficulty, they develop it after new neural networks are formed as they learn the language.[2] However, does that preclude Japanese adults from ever producing and discriminating these sounds? On the contrary, there is evidence that different groups of neural connections are made and strengthened as adults rehearse and begin discriminating between "R" and "L."

But how can I experience a change of my habitual thought patterns?

Though we are creatures of habitual pattern recognition—you were able to access new perspectives every time you got the punchline to a joke or understood the answer to any of the various puzzles encountered throughout this book.

---

* Similarly, at the Massachusetts Institute of Technology, neurophysiologist Mrignaka Sur has shown that brain regions dedicated to audio processing can restructure themselves in order to process visual information. Sur was able to reroute visual signals from the eye to auditory centers in the brains of newborn ferrets. Within a matter of weeks, visual processing was occurring in these auditory centers—though this may have really confused the ferrets at first.

We also experienced new perspectives through the various images we encountered thus far. Look at Figure 17. It's called a Necker cube. Where do you see the front face of the cube?

Figure 17

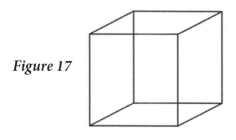

The front face of this cube can be viewed in a couple different ways. It can be seen with the front face protruding out toward the bottom left, or out toward the top right.

Though it is rather difficult to view the cube differently after you've seen it in one way, it is not impossible.

And if you were able to accomplish this, you have just experienced a new perspective first hand.

Figure 18

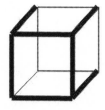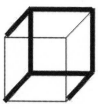

The Story of the Right and Left Hemispheres

Over the years, the relationship between our two cerebral hemispheres and their roles has been interpreted in various ways. Here are a couple of the most popular notions:

- In the majority of people (right-handed), the left hemisphere is dedicated to language processing, while the right is more concerned with interpreting visual and spatial information.
- The right hemisphere is more holistic and the left is only concerned with perceiving the world in discrete parts.

Though the two hemispheres of our brains are not perfectly symmetrical, the popular interpretations are a bit of an over-generalization. We also know that they don't operate like completely separate cities, as several roads connect the two—the largest being the superhighway known as the corpus callosum. Still, there seem to be at least two other ways to interpret the data that not only sheds light on this distinction, but also demonstrates how our brain has built-in mechanisms to think differently.

Literal and Meaning-full Hemispheres

When I was younger, I remember being told numerous times by some authority figure what I could or couldn't do. *You can't run across the street. You can't play ball in the house. You can't eat dessert before supper.*

On my more mischievous days, I'd do my best to find some clever way to get around these restrictions. *So you say I can't eat dessert before my supper? Fine, then I just won't eat supper. Or you say I can't run across the street? Fine, then I'll just run to its center and back home again. That's not running across it.*

I followed the rules. I followed their *exact words*—just maybe not their intent. It was a technique I think I learned from an episode of the Brady Bunch.

In many studies, patients with damage to their right hemisphere display an inability to understand anything other than the *literal meaning* of words.[3] They have problems correctly interpreting figurative and indirect language, such as metaphors, sarcasm, and irony. For instance, imagine asking a coworker if he could have the reports done tomorrow. Those with left hemisphere damage are able to understand this as an indirect request. On the other hand, those with right hemisphere damage are only able to access a literal meaning (*Yes, I can have them done tomorrow*), and cannot figure out that this question is a request in disguise—not that you were trying to be subversive. Such re-evaluation requires multiple perspectives and meanings that are not accessible to them.*

---

*In another study, Ellen Winner and Howard Gardner gave patients pictures and asked them to choose the one that best matched the phrase "to have a heavy heart." Individuals with right hemisphere damage demonstrated more of a tendency to select images that represented a literal interpretation of the phrase than did people without any brain damage.

According to psychologist Robert Ornstein, these studies indicate that the left hemisphere is critical for making literal interpretations of the world. Conversely, it seems that our ability for re-interpretation stems from the right hemisphere's role in maintaining multiple perspectives and holding multiple meanings.[4]

Studies also reveal that patients with right hemisphere damage are often unable to imagine parts as existing within a whole or, in other words, the whole as built up of parts. So for example, a person with right hemisphere damage may have difficulty envisioning arcs as being parts of circles, or envisioning what an *entire* room looks like while standing in the middle of it.[5]

Though this could be interpreted as supporting a holistic-discrete distinction, it could be better interpreted as a distinction between singular and multiple perspectives in light of Ornstein's description of the hemispheres. The patient in the room has difficulty envisioning the entire room because she can only see from one perspective at a time. Without the right hemisphere's ability to maintain multiple meanings and viewpoints, the left hemisphere seems unable to build a larger context for interpreting stimuli. It is stuck with the literal, dominant perspective.

Under this understanding of the hemispheres, I should have known that I wasn't allowed to play in the street under any circumstances, even though I was told specifically, "You can't *run across* the street."

And I probably did know the intent of those instructions.

I just didn't care.

The Novel and Familiar Hemispheres

Brain researcher Elkhonon Goldberg proposes another, yet related theory on hemisphere functions. For fun, let's name the two hemispheres—Left Hemisphere Lawrence and Right Hemisphere Ralph. According to Goldberg, when learning a new task (learning a new instrument, a new language) Ralph does most of the work, but gradually hands it over to Lawrence as the task becomes more familiar.[6] Regardless of the task, Ralph appears to learn new neural connections and firing patterns, and then, these are stored in Lawrence's apartment.

- Visual: In one experiment, patients were shown several pictures of faces. Though the language-visuospatial theorists would have predicted more activity in the right hemisphere, this was only true when the faces were unfamiliar. When viewing familiar faces, it was the left hemisphere that displayed more neural activity.[7]

- Language: With respect to language processing, adults with left hemisphere damage often seem to have impaired linguistic and cognitive problem-solving capabilities, while adults with right hemisphere damage do not. This observation is what has led many to the conclusion that the left hemisphere is responsible for language processing. However, studies also show that children with right hemisphere damage have difficulty with language development. This seems to indicate that the right hemisphere is critical in learning a language initially and only transfers the language processing activity to the left over time.

- Misc: Further research has shown through neuroimaging that the right hemisphere is not just crucial in verbal and visiospatial development, but also in the development of all cognitive tasks regardless of timeframe—whether something is being learned within a matter of hours or years. For example, studies with student musicians demonstrate that the more skilled one becomes, the more the neural activity shifts from the right to left hemisphere.[8]

Evidence also suggests that this interplay between Ralph and Lawrence isn't a consistent division of labor. As we go from childhood to old age, we gradually rely more on Lawrence than we do on Ralph.[9] Poor Ralph doesn't get to exercise his learning chops, while Lawrence stays busy managing our pile of learnt ideas and behaviors.

With neuroplasticity and the relationship between the two hemispheres, it looks like our brains are built for thinking differently. That's kind of encouraging.

The brain can restructure neural networks so that new neural connections can be formed. It also has evolved a specific division of labor between the hemispheres that enables it to grow, learn, adapt, carry multiple meanings, and hold various perspectives. So it definitely appears that we have the inherent capability to think differently.

But the findings also show that over time we tend to rely more on what we've already learned rather than on exercising our faculties for thinking differently. We tend to become more reliant on what's stored in our left hemisphere and disengage the novel perspectives accessible to us through our right. The more we activate particular neural networks, the more ingrained they become. So because we often operate based on learnt habits and perceptions, we end up reinforcing them, making it even more difficult to create new ones.

And we shouldn't forget that habitual pattern recognition, while enabling us to quickly make sense of the world, also confines our perception to our initial, most dominant interpretation of it. In a sense then, we have a propensity for a limited, literal interpretation of the world.

So how do we make use of Ralph's capabilities? What are the actual nuts and bolts of finding new ideas and solutions?

We'll get to that soon. Lots of books and creativity coaches jump right into that discussion, but most of us don't ever get that far in our lives. Too often, we're stuck on the shore, just wanting things to be different. Being well versed in all the idea generating strategies and tricks known to man is no good unless we are able to overcome our self-doubt and accept that creative possibilities exist.

These first issues are also what need to be addressed to lay the groundwork for creativity in group settings. A lack of understanding of what the first two stages entail can undermine successful cooperative creativity. If some of the participants are unwilling to accept that alternatives are possible or lack the hope to think they are worth pursuing, other members will either feel reluctant to explore or unmotivated to participate, and tension may arise that slows down the process and creates unnecessary animosity.

These early stages are important to describe so that we can recognize and prevent them from sabotaging our efforts.

CHAPTER TEN
The Stage of The Martyr

We can take the first steps off of our shores by realizing alternatives exist and are worth investigating. Next, we have to make room for our new perceptions, ideas, and solutions by clearing out space for them.

It is in this stage of the Creative Journey that we descend into the creative underworld. By weakening our dominant neural networks, freeing ourselves of the chains that bind our creativity, we can find ourselves in a much more shadowy world where meaning and perception are up for grabs. It can seem foreboding and dark since we no longer have our firm beliefs and ideas to hold onto for clarity of understanding.

To successfully participate in this stage, we step foot outside the stream of normal procedure, deconstructing the firm associations ingrained in the left hemisphere by challenging assumptions and looking beyond generalizations. We must actually be willing to let go of our old thoughts and patterns of actions.

If we are unwilling to let go of our dominant ideas and behaviors, we are liable to get bogged down at sea.

Challenge Assumptions

I had mentioned in Chapter 2 that fresh eyes have often lead to innovative ideas. However, as we have discovered, fresh eyes are not always easy to come by.

Read the text "new ideas arenowhere." Under normal circumstances, you'd arrive at an interpretation immediately—"new ideas are nowhere"—perhaps. Ask yourself *what if that weren't true?* Or *what other ways can I interpret it?* Once you question your immediate interpretation, you may realize that there is an alternative interpretation available: "new ideas are now here."

One way to attain a new perspective is to get beyond generalizations; to challenge assumptions; and to question rules, paradigms, and ways of doing things. In general, we can list our assumptions and play a game of "What if that weren't true?" or "What if it did not have to be that way?"

You can practice challenging your assumptions by solving the following lateral thinking puzzle:

Imagine one man that is being chased home by another. As he is being chased home, he finds another man waiting for him there with a mask. What could possibly be going on here?

First, try to determine what you are assuming, and then, try to question those assumptions.

(Do not read on if you want a chance to figure this out on your own.)

In order to explore the possible solutions to this puzzle, several preconceptions must be challenged. The creative hero must challenge everything from her notion of a chased man to her notion of men in masks. It is only by freeing herself of these preconceptions that she may eventually determine that the men were all part of a baseball game.

We often have difficulty challenging our assumptions because of the fear of being wrong or of creating bad ideas. In fact, whenever we come up with new ideas and novel ways of doing things, we will inevitably be butting heads with convention. So to fully participate in the exploration of creative possibilities, we must cultivate some sort of pleasure in being wrong.

Many of us grow up believing that being right is of the utmost importance. In order to think differently, being wrong is absolutely necessary, as it allows us to escape old paradigms and exposes us to new ones. It may be worth the trouble to lose an argument, if only temporarily, in order to gain a new perspective. Also, it is a necessary part of the creative process to generate "bad" orchestrations, story plotlines, photographs, color combinations, and mechanical designs on the way to your final creative idea.

By limiting your exploration to only "good" ideas, you access only the field of possibilities allowed by your old assumptions of what is good. By limiting your exploration to only "correct" ideas, you will rarely find novel ones because your assumptions of correctness will rule out most. Your value judgments of good and bad are based upon the current story you use to perceive the world. In order to access new ideas that are outside your current lens of perception, you will undoubtedly have to explore ideas that your current perception will judge as bad or wrong.

We can only learn something new if we dare to venture beyond what we think we know.

The Martyr

The archetype of this stage in the creative process is the martyr. Where the task of the innocent was to become aware of the possibility of a different world and where the orphan was to gain hope that the different world may be fruitful, the martyr's task is to sacrifice the firm concepts and patterns of behavior that helped give her ordinary life meaning.

Our task in the second stage was to cross the Pit of Pessimism. The task in the third is to slay the Dragon of Dominant Ideas and Actions. The dragon seems to follow us around every turn, for preconceptions are difficult to escape. It is as if the ordinary world that the orphan left with trepidation transforms itself into a beast that blocks the martyr's path.

The tendency to stick to our old beliefs and patterns of behavior is evident in all aspects of our lives. Studies have shown that humans have a tendency to stick with those who are like themselves and stray away from those who seem different, with different viewpoints. Some psychologists have labeled this as the "similar-attraction effect."[1] Often, managers hire employees based on this effect and wind up with a less diverse and ultimately less creative workforce. Because repetition strengthens neural connectivity, continually surrounding yourself with like-minded people will make it difficult to form novel ideas and perspectives. This compounds our problem because there is already a gradual shift of activity from the right to left hemisphere as we age, and leaning more on learned knowledge stored here tends to reinforce our dominant networks.

If I dump my old idea, I might feel blue, 'cause letting go is hard to do.
As difficult as slaying the dragon may seem, it is a natural, frequent

occurrence. This is most noticeable in the scientific endeavor. In order to learn anything new, some old belief must pass. All new scientific advancements replace previously held theories, and some of these theories were even referred to as laws prior to their being found obsolete.

Remember, the earth was perceived and believed to be flat before it was proven to be round. And the sun was believed to revolve around the earth before the opposite was found true. We are still struggling to comprehend the relativity of time—that the rate at which one moment passes to the next is relative to one's frame of reference. In other words, the passage of time from moment to moment is not experienced the same by all observers.

Even more astounding is the fall of the Newtonian notion of an absolutely deterministic universe—that there is a cause for every effect. Immediately following the time of Sir Isaac Newton, the dominant train of thought was that deterministic laws of physics governed the actions of all physical entities. Just like the ordinary world of the creative hero, such a paradigm gave many a feeling of security. It meant that things did not happen at random and that the world was predictable as long as we had sufficient information of the present state of things. However, with discoveries in the subatomic realm,* science has come to the conclusion that the material world is inherently probabilistic.[2]

Imagine how weird it would be if a fastball thrown from a pitcher to catcher evaporates in mid flight, leaving no evidence of where it went. Or imagine how unnerving it would be to attend a business meeting and have your clothes suddenly vanish from your body. Believe it or not, this is the sort of thing that happens in the subatomic realm—particles appear to randomly come into and go out of existence, seemingly without cause. This is the epitome of the Creative Journey into the abyss—accepting a world full of uncertainty.

Slaying the Dragon of Dominant Ideas and Actions

So now that we know it is possible to let go of old ideas and behaviors, how do we do it? Is there an off button or an eject lever that I call pull?

*Subatomic realm refers to the world of particles smaller than the atom— e.g., protons, electrons, and neutrons.

Depending on what kind of endeavor you are working on, you have to be keenly aware of what your assumptions are. Do you see only one possible shape to mold your clay into? Do you hear music only in one particular meter or only of a particular orchestration? Do you see only one way to be profitable? Do you see only one way to deal with heart disease?

You have to become aware of why you think you are stuck. You have to ask yourself what it is that is preventing you from moving on. Is it your budget, manpower, time, other responsibilities, materials, your idea of what a good painting looks like, your idea of what productivity means, your idea of what a poem should feel like?

Also, try to be aware of when you are jumping to conclusions or when you feel emotionally tied to an idea or point of view. If you feel like trying to defend a particular perception or a particular method of doing something, that perception may be something to challenge, especially if it halts the examination of new ideas. It may be an assumption to put aside for the time being in order to allow the creative process to explore new avenues.

> Letting go means finding out what it is the dragon is attracted to and then tossing it aside, if only temporarily.

When I began writing this book, my mind was loaded with a plethora of assumptions concerning why I would fail: *I don't have enough experience, I haven't done enough research, I have no time, I have no skills, nobody would be interested in what I had to say etc...* (I better stop there before I convince you to return this book and demand a full refund).

In order to overcome these assumptions, I drove to a nearby beach and just wrote them all down. By doing this, I realized that there weren't as many of them as I had thought and that they were not as bad as I had made them out to be. I then challenged them all and was able to let them go. After doing this, I found myself at a new starting point to reframe my endeavor. I was able to make new associations and find different ways to perceive this undertaking: *I've done tons of research, I've taught and participated in creative activities all my life, everyone could use greater access to possibilities.* I found new meaning for my writing, one in which I felt empowered rather than overwhelmed.

In general though, in order to change our common thought processes, we must not only let go of old ones, but we must learn how to find and play around with new ones. So in order to create new neural networks, we must access new insights and actually generate different associations between ideas—discover new stories to make sense of our experience.

To use a water analogy, part of the process may require us to first empty a bucket of old water in order to fill it up with fresh water. However, like with a broken toilet, we may just need to dump some fresh water into the bowl to flush the old stuff out—a topic that is the central theme of our next chapter.

Summary:

- 3rd Stage: Entering the Sea of Possibilities
- Archetype: The Martyr
- Task: Letting go of Old Behaviors and Preconceptions
- Obstacle: The Dragon of Dominant Ideas and Actions

The 4th Aspect
Trials and Tribulations of Finding New Ideas

The Siren's Song

The beggar noticed that the setting sun was approaching the horizon.

"After confronting the dragon, I felt empowered. I felt free to continue on my journey thinking that nothing could be as scary as a fire-breathing dragon."

"So it was smooth sailing from then on?" asked the laborer. "No other work to be done?"

"Far from it!" replied the beggar. "The majority of my trials and tribulations occurred after my encounter with the dragon. Once I rid myself of all the pickles and doughnuts my boat became lighter. This meant that I began to travel faster west. I had to battle pirates, fierce sea creatures, and vultures. In the process, I had to break off a sharp piece of my boat and use it as a weapon to defend myself. With it, I was able to slice, dice, chop, and toss away what things crossed my path."

"What a grueling experience," said the farmer.

"It was indeed, and I became very tired as a result. But I found that I performed best when I treated it with an explorer's gusto—when I thought less about where I wanted to end up and simply enjoyed this grand adventure I was having away from the island. I was always reenergized when I approached my ordeals in this way—in my own explorer way."

The village drunk then began to babble, barely coherent. "I've lived a life that's full. I've traveled each and every highway."

"Hush," replied the chef.

"Stop your playing around, drunk," added the religious person, "and let the beggar finish."

While the villagers were dismayed by the apparent lack of respect, the beggar enjoyed the sporadic outburst. "Actually, it was when I didn't approach my exploits *my way*—with the soul of a true explorer—that I found myself off course."

The villagers turned their attention away from the drunk and back solely onto the beggar.

"As I was battling my foes, I heard a beautiful voice from across the sea. It was a sweet, soprano tone that seemed to linger in the air just long enough for me to catch it before being swept away by the wind. I became entranced by it. So much so, that I soon realized I had drifted off course and away from the creatures that had blocked my path west."

The villagers' eyes began to wander as if trying to listen to the sounds of the dusk wind as it brushed by their ears.

"What was it saying?" asked the doughnut maker.

"I couldn't tell at first. But, as I continued heading away from the sun's path, I found myself face to face with a gorgeous, young siren in a long, blue silk gown and long, flowing golden hair."

The male villagers' eyes widened, while the female villagers rolled theirs.

"And she hovered in the sky, above my boat. She was close enough for me to hear her words, but too far to touch."

"What was she saying?" asked the chef.

"Well, that was the odd thing. She wasn't saying anything. She was singing. And, as if overcome by a spell, I fell to my knees and listened …

I've heard the news
You're looking around
For hidden treasure
That can't be found.

Your fight with vultures
Will lead nowhere
Sea creatures will continue
To attack and scare.

The winds will blow
Until you wreck.
And then the pirates
Will board your deck.

They say the island's the limit
And to me that's really true.
Go back to pickles and doughnuts
Don't see this journey through.

Because you're bad. You're bad.
Rea—lly bad.
You know you're not good. You're bad.
You know it.

The whole world's gonna answer with a song
To tell you over and over again.
You're bad.

"What a horrific song!" yelled out the doughnut maker.

"You must have been condemned!" cried the religious person.

The laborer shouted, "That must have been some sort of war chant!"

"No!" exclaimed the beggar. "It was not a condemnation or war chant. The siren was trying to censor my activities. You must understand that it is a very arduous path toward the treasure. The siren was simply trying to keep me safe in her own unique way."

The villagers paused to reflect on the beggar's words.

"It sounds like you were kept safe, at least temporarily."

"You had a reprieve from the obstacles at sea."

"And you were privy to the sounds of a beautiful voice."

"Not to mention the sight of a beautiful young lady."

The beggar nodded in agreement. "Yes. Those are all true. But I did not cross the dangerous pit, set sail on a boat, confront a fire-breathing dragon, battle pirates, sea creatures, and vultures simply to encounter an enchantress. I had veered off course, and no matter how entranced I was with the siren, I needed to break free of her spell."

The laborer jumped up into a fighting stance. "So did you pluck her from the sky and slay her with your weapon?"

The chef leaped up and added, "Did you slice her and dice her into tiny pieces?"

"And then," the doughnut maker asked enthusiastically, "did you toss her into the sea, like doughnut dough into hot, burning doughnut oil?"

"No!" the beggar exclaimed. "I did not pluck her, slay her, chop her, or toss her! What is wrong with you people? She wasn't a salad!"

The villagers looked at each other, perplexed by the beggar's response.

"What's a salad?" asked the religious person.

"Never mind that...I did no such vulgar acts like the ones you all have suggested."

"So what did you do?" asked the chef.

"I simply acknowledged her, thanked her for sharing her tune, and then I did my best to block out her voice. I had to sing my own song in order to filter out hers from my awareness. Only by doing this could I keep my focus on my travels west."

The laborer was curious. "What song did you sing?"

"Was it some spiritual hymn?" asked the religious person.

"Actually, I sang the following over and over again to myself..." and the beggar began to sing the poetic lyrics of the most marvelous song the villagers had ever heard.*

Then, at the end, he completed his performance with the most heart-felt words. "Sha na na na na na na na, sha na na na na. Sha na na na na na na na, sha na na na na."

The farmer began to applaud. "What a magical tune!"

"Only a sophisticated aria such as this could have possible countered the siren's mesmerizing serenade," said the religious person.

"Yes, and I was once again able to head west. Singing this song was the only way for me to once again become an explorer—to be myself again, rather than a stagnant listener of that enchantress."

The villagers sat back down and looked at the beggar in amazement.

"For what's a man? What's he got? If not himself, then he has naught," spoke the beggar.

"True!" replied the villagers in unison.

"To say what he truly feels and not the drivel of one who kneels. History shows I took the blows," continued the beggar.

"Sea creatures, pirates, and vultures," the villagers all commented.

The beggar nodded in agreement. "Yes. And when push came to shove, I did it my way."

---

*As of the publication of this book, it was too expensive to pay for permission to reprint the lyrics to this song (yes, it is a real song). I encourage you to find them yourself online by searching for "Time to Change" performed by the Brady Bunch. I think you'll find it enlightening...or at least mildly amusing.

CHAPTER ELEVEN

The Not-So-Secret Secrets to Out-of-the-Box Thinking

Scenario 2: There is a carrot, a pile of pebbles, and a pipe lying together in the middle of a field. Why?

For some of you, this is the chapter you've been waiting for. You may have read the back cover, read the introduction, or attended one of my workshops and heard me speak of the "Secrets to Out-of-the-Box Thinking." In fact, you may have just ran across this book on the shelf of a bookstore and immediately jumped to this chapter wanting to know what The Secrets are.

I also know from my research that there are a number of you who are natural wizards at coming up with new ideas. You are the type that easily comes up with crazy notions and off-the-wall concepts, and maybe, your difficulty is turning them into a reality. This dilemma is addressed in the 6th aspect of the creative process. However, though the secrets of this 4th aspect may not seem so secret to you, I hope you'll find here a new way to envision how you come up with new ideas. And as we've already explored, new perspectives can often lead to even more creative insights.

Where did these creative thinking secrets come from?

These "Not-so-Secret" secrets to out-of-the-box thinking are the basic "techniques" and strategies that I have found most common in books on creative, out-of-the-box, and lateral thinking. Authors use different terms or write for specific audiences (writer, painter, businessperson, entrepreneur, inventor), and this can make them sound different. But I've done my best here to describe them in general enough terms to make them applicable to anyone—even good old

Uncle Max who seems stuck in his ways.

These secrets are the closet ways to be creative "on-demand." These secrets allow you to actively participate in the story building needed to make sense out of life's many conundrums, including the one that began this chapter.

Such issues call for optimal solutions and not absolute, calculable answers. They require us to reinterpret our initial perceptions of the scenario and of what is possible through the use of our creative faculties. And the solutions often occur as flashes of insight.

The secrets in this chapter are ways to access a larger breadth of ideas and are the beginning steps to becoming more "insight prone."

The Secrets to Exploring New Ideas

Wait a minute. If creative insights and new ideas come as flashes from the unconscious, why do we have to actively try to do anything?

As Freud once said, "When inspiration does not come to me, I go halfway to meet it."

You can think of this active process as warming up the mind for insight. All these activities engage our dominant ideas, our dominant patterns of thought, and try to loosen them. They also promote a mental environment where our unconscious can have more freedom to roam and where we can actually be in a state of mind to perceive its ruminations rather than block it by the over-activity of our conscious thoughts and common neural patterns.

To be more susceptible to experiencing creative insights it may be better to search in new streams rather than try to fish for them in our old ones.

Here we participate in creative play—making associations between new ideas—in order to not only come across insights (which our unconscious often does), but also to further weaken the barricades posted by our conditioned perceptions. We play around with new ideas or with altering old ones. It's here that the artist doodles, the musician plays around with sounds, the inventor tinkers, and the scientist dreams of the hypothetical. As I like to say, the organization that brainstorms together goes beyond the norms together.

Such creative play is the meat of ingenuity and inventiveness. By actively exploring like children, we can make ourselves more susceptible to the flashes of genius that can help us deal with the scenarios of our adult lives. It is through this type of exploration that you may have been led to the idea that the carrot, pebble, and pipe from scenario 2 were all remnants of a melted snowman.

There are numerous specific strategies for creative play in various different endeavors. There are specific activities that the painter, the engineer, the salesman, the financial analyst, the clothing designer, the photographer, the dancer, and the business group can participate in to loosen their minds and explore new ideas. But, for the most part, they all follow many of the basic approaches discussed below.

You were born with the faculties for creative play. So here are the secrets to helping you *remember* how to do just that.

Secret #1: Go with the Flow

Have you ever been wowed by a great jazz improviser, comedic improviser, or extemporaneous speaker? In jazz, virtuosos like Ella Fitzgerald, Bobby McFarrin, Charlie Parker, and Dizzy Gillespie wow the crowd with their extemporaneous outpouring of creativity. On the spot, they are able to improvise a melody that nobody has ever heard anywhere at anytime. The same is true of a comedy improvisation troupe that plays a "theater game" and—based upon random suggestions from the audience—creates novel scenes and dialogue on the spur of the moment.

For the audience listening and watching these improvisational performances, the quality of these extemporaneous performances can be mind-boggling and magical.

How can they come up with that out of thin air?

One short answer is that they all *went with the flow.*

Do you think such improvisational feats are beyond your abilities? If you said yes, guess again, and ask yourself this: when was the last time you caught yourself daydreaming? I won't be offended if you were daydreaming while reading this book. It would actually make me very happy.

Try to remember what that felt like. You started thinking about one thing, and that led you to another thing, which led you to another, and so on. Like being caught by the stream of a river, you were carried along a free flowing stream of ideas. Before you knew it, a simple thought about tomorrow's board meeting led you to realize how amazing a glass of strawberry lemonade would taste right after making-out with your lover (I'll let you fill in the blanks on that one).

So what happened when I daydreamed?

When we daydream, we let go of needing to control our thoughts. We allowed one thought to naturally, organically lead us to another without consciously directing where they went.

Nancy Andreasen, neuroscientist and psychiatrist, noticed that much of our creative thoughts occurred this way: randomly, without our conscious direction. To understand the anatomy of these thoughts, Andreasen performed a study that used a PET scan to monitor blood flow to the brain. Under one condition, subjects consciously directed their thoughts by recalling the events of their day. In another, the subjects were asked to close their eyes and rest in the attempt to encourage less directed thoughts.

The results showed that during the rest condition almost all activity was located in the association cortex. If you recall, they are the folks in our brain's different "districts" whose only job is to communicate with other districts—like the person in the financial district whose sole job it is to communicate with the restaurant folks, the government folks, and so on. They are unspecialized and not pre-wired for anything other than being the bridge between our brain's different lobes.

What Andreasen's study indicates is that the association cortex plays an important part not only in the integration of information between brain regions, but also in producing a good amount of the activity often associated with the unconscious mind. She goes on to make the following observations:

> It is as if the multiple association cortices are communicating back and forth...simply in response to one another. These associations are occurring freely. They are running unchecked.... Initially these associations may seem meaningless or unconnected.... Out of this disorganization, self-organization eventually emerges and takes over in the brain. The result is a completely new and original thing: a mathematical function, a symphony, or a poem.[1]

To increase the activity of the association cortex, Andreasen suggests the use of free association thinking. It is what occurs when you daydream. You simply let your mind wander and see what ideas and notions float into your awareness. As they come in, you allow them to lead you to other ideas and then to others. Your thoughts are meant to come in undirected without your consciousness stirring them in toward particular places. Also, your thinking must be open-ended without a predetermined end point. By exercising undirected, open-ended thinking, we may be able to form new associations and be privy to more creative insights.

For example, during a great jazz improvisation, the improviser hears what the band is playing, which leads her to start performing the first few notes of a new melody, and the constant interaction inspires her further. The same goes for the comedic improviser.

Are you saying we should daydream to be creative?

To think creatively, we need to daydream about our ideas, perceptions, and concepts playfully without any goal in mind. Become an observer. Try not to participate by controlling the movement of your thoughts. This is one of the reasons brainstorming can be useful because we have no control over what somebody else is going to say. The idea with brainstorming is to generate as many ideas as possible. So the focus is on quantity as opposed to quality. In other words, we want to have access to as diverse an intersection of ideas as possible.

In order to do this, we need to let go of the need to be critical and instead embrace all ideas, especially uncommon ones. For instance, in all of the above examples, the participants must "play off" of the current ideas. If you're free-associating by yourself, you take your current idea, accept it, and play off of it without question. If you're free-associating with others (brainstorming, jazz improvisation, theater improvisation), you play off of each other's ideas without denying them. In fact, this a major commandment of theater improvisation:

Thou shall not negate other people's statements. Just add on to them.

In short: Agree. Accept. Add.

Imagine you're asked to improvise a scene about being out with a friend on a Sunday afternoon. Your fellow actor begins by saying, "Hey Sarah, isn't it great being out here hiking in the woods?"

And you respond: "Woods? What woods? We're in a bowling alley?"

That's a sure fire way of becoming the most hated actor in your troupe. You stopped the scene before it really even started. If the two of you just kept negating each other, the scene would never get the chance to develop, and the improvised story would never go anywhere.

So the principle behind going with the flow is to allow your thoughts to take you to places without your active participation. The first idea or thought that comes up may not be the solution to your problem. However, if left alone it may inspire or lead you to another idea which could lead to a third one and so on until you stumble upon your 'aha' moment. The initial idea may only be the first step on a lateral path to an invaluable insight.

Secret #2: Mix & Match—Combinatory Play

"Step into the stream." That's another way of making yourself more flexible to new ideas. Randomly explore new combinations of 'old' ideas, perceptions, and concepts. Einstein was able to arrive at so many unique ideas concerning the nature of the universe by such combinatory play.

And just like Einstein, you participate in combinatory play anytime you mix and match your furniture, dishes for dinner (pasta and apple pie), and items on your desk at work. You participate in combinatory play every time you mix and match your clothes and accessories.

Whenever you mix and match anything, you are like Einstein. But don't let that get to your head.

Here are a couple more examples of rather well known mix and matches.

- Abstract expressionist painters participated in combinatory play when they used house paint brushes, basting syringes, and trowels to create works of art. Further, they experimented with drips, splatters, and accidental marks by throwing and squirting paint, not very conventional ways of creating a painting.[2]
- The results of combinatory play need not be so abstract. The British rock band Queen combined rock-and-roll with opera

and produced the hit song *Bohemian Rhapsody*.

- Author Bernard Malamud combined baseball with the quest for the Holy Grail and created the novel and movie *The Natural*.

But what if I can't think of any new mixes and matches?

Instead of waiting for these sorts of unique associations to present themselves, you can also intentionally rearrange the associations of *what you already know*. For instance, if you're looking to improve a process or a plan, you can write out all the steps of your current process and try rearranging them.

- A company can look at their production flow and rearrange the order of the process.
- An entrepreneur can look at the typical chain of events that occurs when buying a burrito and decide she could be more efficient by changing the order around (Chipotle anyone?).
- A painter can rearrange the colors and shapes of an earlier work to create something new.
- A screenwriter can decide to start their movie at the middle or end of their story and end the movie at its beginning.
- Or a musician can take a melody and rearrange the order that she plays the notes.

In other words, you take the chain of ideas associated with whatever you're looking to change, and then, just rearrange the chains. You'll definitely arrive at some interesting ideas that may or may not be useful, but they could possibly inspire you and open up paths towards ones that are.

The idea is to simply allow yourself to *play* around with unconventional idea combinations for the sake of exploration and not because you feel the need to arrive at a destination.

Secret #3: Random Stimulation

If you're still having trouble exciting creative neural networks, you can let the external world excite them for you. You can do this through a technique called *random stimulation*. I know to some it sounds like another of my double entendres, but I can't take credit for this one. It really is a term frequently found in creative thinking circles. So there is no need to be afraid. It's safe, easy, and you don't have to feel guilty about it afterwards.

What is random stimulation?

Here's the scoop: have you ever had an idea just come to you out of the blue based on something somebody else said or something that quickly caught your eye? Well, you're not alone. And as it turns out, many creative individuals make this sort of random stimulation a part of their creative process.

- George Harrison decided he would write a song based on the first book he saw at his mother's house. At random, he picked a book and found the phrase "gently weeps." He would go on to quickly write the popular Beatles song *While My Guitar Gently Weeps*.

- Edgar Allan Poe also used random stimulation strategies. For example, to come up with a plot for his next tale, he would randomly pick words out of the dictionary and attempt to associate them into a story. If an idea struck him, he would begin writing, and if not, he would simply find a new batch of words.

Random stimulation is the engine that drives many comedy improvisational games. Here, the theater troupe calls upon the audience to provide random suggestions that form the basis of their game. For instance, my comedy troupe often plays a game called *Mr. Wikipedia*. While on stage, we solicit "tough" questions from the audience that we will attempt to answer as one "mind"—i.e., as Mr. Wikipedia.

Here's how the game works. First, we decide on the order that each of us will speak. And when it comes time to answer the question, each member of the troupe speaks in that order, adding one word at a time to the answer until a sentence is formed. So let's say, Tom, Becky (fictitious names to protect the innocent), and I receive a quirky question from the audience such as, "Where can I find a leprechaun?"

This is what may occur…

Javy: You
Tom: can
Becky: find

Javy: leprechauns
Tom: in
Becky: Kenny
Javy: Rogers
Tom: beard!

Not only are we soliciting random stimulation from the audience, but each troupe member must respond to random stimulation from the troupe member who spoke before them, like when brainstorming. We may not always be funny, and frequently aren't, but it almost always generates a unique association of ideas.

How can I apply random stimulation to my creative endeavors?

You can apply random stimulation in various different ways depending on your endeavor. The creative entrepreneur may sit at a coffee shop and listen to random conversations to discover what inconveniences could be helped by a new product or service. The visual artist may blindly pick out a color from a box of crayons. The unhappy employee may randomly walk around town or browse through a random magazine to find inspiration for a new career. You could roll a pair of dice, pick a card from a deck, peruse a museum, invite input from random people, or throw darts at a poster or a map. Random inspiration can come from anywhere and from anything.

If you haven't already noticed, it's really just free-associating. But instead of doing it by yourself or within a particular group, you're free-associating with *anything* you choose. You can free-associate with the world at large.

So when you feel as if your internal well is dry, an unlimited supply of random stimulation awaits you in the external world.

Secret #4: Expand Representations through Reframing

We saw in Chapter 3 how our perceptions are often shaped by the way information is framed. For instance, the phrases *93% survival rate* and *7% mortality rate* convey the same facts but elicit very different responses.

For this reason, like a home buyer who stops by a potential home at different times of the day or an interior designer who looks at their decorations while varying the room's luminosity, you'll often find it useful to reframe a scenario in order to see it in a different light.

Change Your Modes of Thinking

One way to reframe a perspective is to change the mode in which you are experiencing it. For instance, if you are thinking about a scenario in words or equations, you may want to try visualizing it instead. Rather than thinking about the nature of light in terms of scientific language or mathematical equations, Einstein arrived at his insights by visualizing riding a light beam through space.

When I taught high school music, one of the most difficult things to do was teach an ensemble how to play soft, or *pianissimo*. It was often useful to provide them with a visual representation, where I would use the distance between my hands to express dynamics. It also helped to have them think of dynamics as a scale from 1 to 10 so they could envision where pianissimo was relationally rather than rely on an abstract cry of "play soft!"

Analogy and Metaphor

A direct way to reframe a perspective is to rephrase it through an analogy. An analogy allows you to present what you know in an alternate language allowing you to think through your knowledge. It could be envisioning your wealth as a plant that you need to grow, or seeing the invention you are working on as a baby you are caring for, or thinking of creativity as a heroic journey. It could also be thinking of your employees as team members or envisioning a social problem as an economic one.

As I have been advocating throughout this book, trying to see your scenario in different terms may expose new associations of ideas, new choices to explore, or new approaches to your endeavor. By perceiving your portfolio like a plant, you may finally see that building wealth requires time, nurturing, and constant feeding. By thinking of your employees as team members, you may find their dissenting ideas as valuable as their manpower and that morale improves performance.

Choreographer Twyla Tharp has even used coins to represent her dancers, tossing the coins in the air and using the resulting patterns to inspire her dance formations. This is an example of combining the reframing of a problem with random stimulation for ideas.

The effectiveness of reframing is one of the reasons why teaching tales and metaphors are such an effective education tool. Using literal, declarative statements usually trigger our dominant perceptions. Through an analogy, we can see things *as if*. Investigating our scenarios through the terms of a metaphor may not trigger our dominant perceptions and reactions so quickly. This then helps us avoid the limitations of our habitual pattern recognition. We can then deepen the meaning of what we are learning, often through the new imagery provided by the metaphor.

For example, when your mother tells you that life is unpredictable, you may have a particular literal understanding of those words. And it may be that she's told you this so often that you have grown numb to it, unable to get any more value from her words. But you may be privy to a new perception when she tells you that life is like a box of chocolates—i.e., it can be bitter, sweet, crunchy, soft, or pure ecstasy. *You never know what you're gonna get.*

In order to find creative approaches to your art, business, or life, you can try replacing the lens through which you perceive these things. You could try to find a new story with which to make sense out of your experience. By doing so, new connections between ideas can appear that were not obvious through the old lens of perception.

Secret #5: Being a Little Nutty

This secret is short, sweet, and all about attitude.

Deviating from normal thinking processes requires us to be unafraid of being weird, unusual, or a bit nutty. We need to go beyond our ideas of normalcy in order to explore novel possibilities. Imagine yourself as the mad scientist with crazy hair, like Doc Brown from the movie *Back To The Future*.

This secret is all about how you approach this stage of your creative endeavor. Be aware of your mindset and personality here. Are you serious? Are you uptight? Are you grumpy? Or are you loose and free, without a care in the world, willing to try anything once?

Why can it be hard for some people to be a little nutty?

The difficulty is that we often live our lives trying to maintain a certain persona. Whether we are aware of it or not, we wear masks in different environments, amongst different groups of people in order to fit in. You can simply reflect on how you and your coworkers behave in the office versus how you might behave in front of your children versus how you might behave when amongst your old school friends. For us adults, we often spend a majority of our time behind a mask of seriousness or one of proper behavior—whatever that might mean. We can get so used to wearing these masks that it can become very difficult to embody a screwball attitude.

This is why in group settings, it may be beneficial to have at least one person who isn't afraid to be wild with their input, throwing in ideas from *left field*. If quantity of ideas is what we are after in this stage, then a wacky approach to the scenario, project, or problem may just be what is needed. It isn't so much that you're relying on them for the creative insight you're after, but that their off the wall ideas may inspire others.

This means you should embrace having a designated oddball, off the wall, crazy Uncle Charlie voice in your group. Better yet, it means appreciating having a little crazy Uncle Charlie in you.

Secret # 6: Don't Worry, Be Happy

Try to bring to mind a moment when you were upset, angry, or depressed.

If you're having trouble, perhaps you can try to recall what your thoughts were like when you were cut off on the freeway, were criticized by your boss, or when you ended a relationship.

Were you preoccupied with your sadness or anger? Did it consume you? It can often be hard to let these emotions go. We often have a tendency to hold onto them, and consequently, we tend to hold onto whatever picture of the world supports those emotions.

Aren't the best artists the ones who are in deep pain?

The "creative type" is often imagined to be the person who seems to live their life in this sort of eternal agony or despair. There are numerous examples of the creative artist who are inspired by their misery or use it as fuel, including songwriters, novelists such as Earnest Hemingway, and a plethora of poets including Sylvia Plath and Emily Dickinson.

However, rather than thinking of negative emotion as the common trait among artists, it may be more accurate to say that emotionality can be great creative fodder in general, whether it be the anger inspired lyrics of a woman scorned or the painting or poetry of a lover who has fallen head over heals in love.

In general though, studies indicate that creativity does indeed favor more positive states of mind. Feelings of joy and love appear to have a much more positive effect on creative output than do feelings of fear, anger, or sadness.[3]

The reason, as you've probably already guessed, is pretty simple. When we are unhappy, we often get stuck or fixated on our issues. We see the world as constricting. We inherently narrow our focus onto limited possibilities. On the other hand, the happier we are, the more open we are to seeing the world as one full of potential and promise. It is this vision that provides the motivation for our optimism.

It is this optimism that can fuel our need to enter and explore the sea of possibilities.

Secret #7: Establish an Exploratory Environment

Sometimes, creative ideas emerge when we are surrounded by inspirational art, music, or by nature through random stimulation.

At other times, we can arrive at creative ideas by being in a nice quiet space without visual distractions, allowing for flashes of creative insights. We'll discuss this in the 5th aspect.

Further, our earlier observations of the creative landscape showed us that we could actively pursue creative ideas by immersing ourselves in a diversity of perceptions giving us access to a wider pool of ideas. We can then be in a better position to challenge assumptions, rearrange associations, or find new analogies. Our free association can then span an even greater breadth. In other words, we can have a larger net to cast in the sea of possibilities.

What's the easiest way to diversify my perceptions?

The quickest way to do this is by immersing ourselves in an environment of diverse individuals. Yet, as anyone who has ever been in any sort of meeting knows, just having diverse individuals doesn't guarantee creative ideas. Instead, it often means a lot of disagreeing, a lot of head shaking, a lot of sighing, and a lot of clock watching.

Luckily, a lot of people, smarter than I, have done research to help us all foster creative groups. Based on this research, here are some key tactics for enhancing group creativity.

The 5 Keys to Unlocking Creativity in Groups

1. Focus on creative environments, not creative people.

A common perception about creative groups is that, in order to be successful, it needs to be filled with creative people. But, as I've been emphasizing, we are all creative. The problem is giving people the freedom and support to exercise it in front of others. In one case, innovative groups were studied to see what the critical factors were for their improvisational capabilities.[4] Rather than individual creative spontaneity, it was the quality of relationship between the group members that emerged as the key factor.

2. Develop trust and comfort.

Oftentimes, when we participate in group projects, we can find ourselves worrying so about how we come across to others that we are unable to relax and simply play around with ideas. What we need to have is trust that our crazy ideas will be appreciated before they are judged. We need to have trust that our group members aren't going to call us names or ridicule us. With this trust and comfort, we can relax enough to simply play around with ideas.

3. Agree. Accept. Add.

In studies that look at brainstorming in groups, the biggest obstacle to creativity seems not to be the lack of creativity or creative individuals, but self-censorship. While many brainstorming courses expertly teach techniques for arriving at unique ideas, brainstorming and other similar group strategies are much more affected by individual psychology. One way to address this is to prepare individuals for the possible negative feedback that they may receive. However, it can also be addressed by limiting the feedback received.[5]

It may just be best to stick with the theater improvisation rule: Agree. Accept. Add.

4. Not I, but We.

This also implies then that it may be beneficial to remove any reward for "coming up" with creative ideas in group brainstorming sessions. A look at several creative companies, such as IDEO, reveals that it can be helpful to shift focus from the individual to the collective.[6] Rather than think of a creative idea as having originated from a specific individual, within group settings, it may be best to think of the idea as the result of a group process of which the individual is a member. It's only fair since the idea of brainstorming is that ideas from one person can help inspire ideas in the next. So truly, they are the result of a collaborative process and not the lone genius.

5. Creative leadership = cultivator of creative environments.

It is for this reason that group facilitators, or managers, shouldn't carry the burden of being the originator of creative ideas but be the caretaker of creative space. During a two-day colloquium of leading scholars and executives from companies, such as Google, IDEO, Novaris, Intuit and E Link, creativity researchers Teresa Amabile and Mukti Khaire concluded that leaders should be responsible for encouraging ideas and cultivating an environment for creativity rather than necessarily being the source of ideas.[7] Likewise, research indicates that group creativity is much less about managing creative individuals and more about providing the right social context and cultivating creative interactions.[8]

Overwhelmed by the Sea of Possibilities

You've done it. You are now part of the select fraternity of individuals that hold the seven secrets to out-of-the-box thinking. You're an official Secret Keeper.*

Now, you're ready to start your conquest of the creative underworld!

What do I do when I find myself overwhelmed by the field of possibilities? It can seem so endless that I don't know where to start or how to jump into the creative intersection.

That can be a problem.

Well, here's where constraints may be helpful. You can arbitrarily set constraints on your exploration to give yourself boundaries to play within. It's like telling somebody, "Go paint!" If that's all the instruction given, one can be overwhelmed with all the possibilities of what that can mean: *Paint what? Paint where?* The same is true for trying to find a new business idea, writing a new poem, or tackling homelessness. For

---

*I don't think that's related to an inn keeper or a goal keeper in soccer, but it's empowering just the same.

our painting example, the painter can set boundaries, such as limiting themselves to a particular canvas and paint set. The poet can constrain themselves to a particular topic, to a certain number of lines, or to a particular meter.

Oftentimes, the boundaries are inherent in your endeavor. You may have a limited budget with which to address homelessness in your community. Or maybe, you wish to find people shelter before wintertime, so you inherently have a timeline to think of a creative solution.

So when you're frozen, stuck, and staring in awe at all the possible directions in which you can steer your ship, start your exploration by simply choosing a certain area of the sea.

Wow. So I guess I am ready to begin my creative conquests.

Yes. But a word of caution, if you're new to all of this, there's a good possibility that some of your creative muscles have atrophied from lack of use. It may be good to exercise them into shape.

Take a look at the next chapter to find out how.

CHAPTER TWELVE
Exercising Our Creative Muscles

Homer wasn't a runner, but he got so excited one day about running a marathon that he decided to buy a book about it. It told him how to breathe, how to swing his arms, how to position his head, and how to strike the ground with his foot. It told him how to drink and eat before, after, and during a race.

After reading the book, Homer thought he was all set. He thought he knew everything he needed to know to run a marathon.

But then, when he went out to try his hand at a simple five-mile run, he wound up just running one.

One tenth of a mile, that is.

He was bewildered. *Was it my shoes?*

Your Creativity Workout Plan

I'm not big into working out. Is a creativity workout difficult?

I hate special diets and training regiments as much as the next guy. However, if we aren't in shape to use our strategies, our strategies become useless. At least in our case, our creative muscles are fun to exercise and our nutritional options are mighty tasty. There's no need to do boring squat thrusts or have skimpy meals consisting of one brussel sprout and a lima bean (no offense to those that love squat thrusts or lima beans). In fact, you'll be doing the opposite. You'll be given permission to indulge in pleasures that you may otherwise feel guilty doing!

So here's the premise:

- If we don't use it, we lose it. Unfortunately, we tend to rely more on our learned concepts and behaviors as we age, and we just end up strengthening our dominant neural networks.

Left hemisphere Lawrence does most of the work, while right hemisphere Ralph becomes a couch potato.

- Studies show that there is significantly more activity in the right hemisphere when we're creative, than when we are not. So, we better find some ways to get Ralph up and running again.
- Luckily, there are some activities we can participate in that specifically give Ralph a workout.

In order to exercise our creative thinking faculties, a conscious effort must be made to actively engage Ralph in everyday life. So, in addition to participating in creative endeavors or engaging in the idea generating activities described previously, give your creative muscles a workout through the following exercises. Mix and match as you please. Just go with the flow and do whichever of these makes you happy. You'll benefit regardless.

Stories

Pick up a fun book with an intriguing story and have a good time. There's no need to feel guilty about wasting time or not "learning" anything new from it.

Remember, right hemisphere Ralph is really important in prosody and non-literal interpretation. It's no surprise then that research indicates it can be exercised through activities requiring extensive exploration of multiple meaning and the use of imagination.

In one study, subjects were given folktales and technical materials to read. While reading the folktales, the right hemisphere appeared much more active than when reading the technical materials.[1] Comparable results were obtained for subjects reading wisdom stories. Reading stories exercises the intellectual faculties needed for thinking differently since they invite us to hold multiple meanings through non-literal interpretation—a function of the right hemisphere.

Silence

It's okay just to hangout without saying a word. You may want to give yourself some alone time to do this, but you may even want to practice being silent while amongst people. They may even thank you for it.

Participating in activities nonverbally has been shown to suppress left hemisphere activity. In a broad sense, suppressing left hemisphere activity may help reduce the activation or priming of our dominant neural networks. It's like turning down the volume on our conscious mind. If we turn down the constant chatter that usually occupies our minds, we may be left with more mental space to make creative associations.

Games and Improvisational Activities

All work and no play makes Ralph a very weak and unhappy brain hemisphere.

Any activity or game that exercises our imagination—exercises our meaning-making skills—can give our creative faculties a workout. These not only include lateral thinking puzzles, but also board games, crossword puzzles, improvisational theater games, unchoreographed dancing, musical improvisation, and a whole host of other activities too numerous to mention. Not only do these activities exercise our ability to generate multiple perspectives and ideas, but they also help to cultivate a playful, fun attitude towards the creative process. As we've seen, we are most creative when we explore ideas like young children. What better way to cultivate this approach than to *practice* being like children?

Also, earlier I mentioned how creativity in groups was very dependent on establishing a creative environment—an environment of trust and comfort. This has led some researchers to believe that games are a key aspect to any group interaction. Through games, groups can develop the comfort and trust necessary to explore the wacky and off the wall. And it's a great way to improve your happiness quotient.

Jokes

Speaking of happiness quotient, you'd be hard pressed to have a bad time while you're exercising your sense of humor. It's a great way to get Ralph excited. However, having a sense of humor means more than simply having the ability to laugh. Though many parts of the brain are involved in processing a joke, research has shown that it is Ralph's ability for new thought, new interpretations, and non-literal thinking that gives the punch line its proper meaning. So crack a joke.

Have you heard the one about the road trip to Disneyland?

> After several years of listening to his children's pleas, a father finally decides to take his family on a road trip to Disneyland. On the third day of their trip, the family finally arrives in Los Angeles. Upon exiting the freeway, the father notices a large street sign, "Disneyland Left."
>
> Disappointed, he turns the car around and drives home.

The punch line, "Disappointed, he turns the car around and drives home," becomes humorous only if the alternative meaning for "Disneyland Left" is accessed. Unfortunately, patients with right hemisphere damage wouldn't see what's funny because they are denied the alternative interpretation.

Cultivating a sense of humor is, in short, cultivating the ability to find multiple meanings and multiple perspectives, a task heavily dependent on right hemisphere Ralph. When we find something to be funny, we are simply re-interpreting information in a context different than the dominant one. So, cultivating a sense of humor will exercise our creative thinking faculties.

Janusian Thinking

What's Janusian thinking?

1. Remember the image of the white vase and black face silhouettes (see Figure 12, Chapter 3, page 78).
2. Or the image of the black dots and spotted dog (see Figure 8, Chapter 3, page 75).
3. Or the puzzle with the men who died in their cabin in the woods (see Chapter 4, page 82).

If you were able to switch your perceptions in these cases, you were participating in Janusian Thinking—seeing opposites as two sides of a coin or two aspects of a greater whole. You were able to hold two opposite perspectives concurrently—a vase and not a vase; silhouettes and not silhouettes; a dog and not a dog (only black dots); a log cabin and not a log cabin. Depending on the context you choose, any of these perceptions are valid.

In fact, this entire book is full of examples of Janusian Thinking.

Can you think of any others?

Often we need to hold on to just one side of the story because we have difficulty dealing with ambiguity. Ambiguity means "we aren't certain," and not being certain about where to find food and where the dangerous tigers were meant that Caveman Fred had reason to worry.

Nevertheless, holding ambiguity is critical to accessing multiple meanings, which Ralph loves to do, but freaks Lawrence out. Ambiguity allows us to see what's out there in the sea of possibilities, which is often what makes venturing out there so scary.

Starting Your Training

Exercising Ralph is fun. You are actually allowing yourself to indulge in so-called 'trivial or wasteful activities' like spending time reading stories or joking. But these fun activities are critical to cultivating your creative muscles. Maybe, you're thinking about beginning a workout plan, worried that it'll be tough to incorporate them into your hectic day. At least, you can rest assured that starting it won't be an issue. If you haven't noticed, you've been participating in all of these exercises from page one of this book.

CHAPTER THIRTEEN
The Stage of Wandering

After emptying ourselves of our old ideas and habits, we must walk towards inspiration by first passing through the stage of Trials and Ordeals. It is in this stage that we explore new connections between ideas—the artist plays around with shapes and colors, the author plays around with plot lines, and the corporation brainstorms new ways to improve profitability. It is here that we step into the intersection, free associate, and access new ideas through random stimulation. The right hemisphere is encouraged to roam free, looking beyond literal perception and initial face value meanings. It is also here that we attempt to fill ourselves up with the creative spirit.

Dance choreographer Twyla Tharp refers to this process as *scratching*, as she digs around her mind and her environment for new ideas for a new show. It is through this process that she creates new choreography—improvising movement and finding bits to combine into larger ideas.

> The first steps of a creative act are like groping in the dark: random and chaotic, feverish and fearful, a lot of busy-ness with no apparent or definable end in sight.[1]

Musicians, poets, and painters also go through a similar process when creating their art. Musicians explore new lines, riffs, hooks, licks, sounds, keys, and instruments in order to find something that may be further developed into something that resonates with them.

- Jazz great John Coltrane became famous as a tenor saxophone player in the 50's and 60's. However, he delved into new realms playing the soprano sax, an instrument that had not really been in use since a few decades earlier. As a result, he went on to create some of his most memorable recordings playing the soprano.

- T.S. Elliot's famous poem *The Waste Land* was the culmination of hundreds of variations.
- Picasso had *scratched* sketches in no less than 8 notebooks in the process of creating his painting, *Les Demoiselles d'Avignon*.

In writing this book, I spent months and months playing around with its structure, its organization, and its content. I went back and forth with different titles, different subtitles, and different chapter names. I spent even more time experimenting with the format of the paragraphs, sentence structure, different metaphors, different analogies, and different word choices until I finally settled on the ones you currently have in your hands.

We are wanderers in this stage, exploring and identifying new forms, participating in combinatory play, and delving into new behaviors for their own sake. Here, the quantity of ideas is treasured more than their quality. Mozart, Bach, and Beethoven created numerous compositions that are not played today, and most of Einstein's papers are not referenced by any other scientist. Dean Simonton, a psychologist at UC Davis, performed research that indicated that most scientists and innovators produced their most insightful work during the periods when they also produced their most mediocre work.[2]

Our challenge here is not necessarily to find anything in particular. Rather, our obstacle is the Siren of Censorship. Judgment is a provocative temptress. It is during this stage of the Creative Journey that we need to overcome the propensity to judge ideas as being good or bad. Writers often speak of how they need to let their creative spirit flow while putting aside their editor voice. In this stage, our greatest challenge is to resist the siren's call and instead continue to generate as many new ideas as we can.

To do this, we need to have two very important attributes.

- First, we need to approach this endeavor with a sense of play, explore for the sake of exploring.
- Secondly, we also need to *feel as if* we have time to wander. Many movies give the impression that creativity and ingenuity are heightened during time-pressured situations. However, Harvard creativity researcher Teresa Amabile performed

experiments that showed time pressure to be detrimental to creativity. Her explanation was that time was needed to postpone judgment of new ideas and review multiple perspectives.[3]

Our sense of humor and a lighthearted approach to our endeavors will help us in this respect.

But isn't it good to judge and critically look at an idea in order to determine its value or its accuracy?

Critical evaluation of ideas is necessary but not at this stage. Judging is absolutely necessary for creating something of quality but again at later stages in the process when you are trying to manifest your creative idea. Here, you won't produce anything unless you first give yourself room to find the ideas for your creative endeavor.

When writing this book, I could have easily gotten bogged down in making sure every word, phrase, and sentence was perfect. At times, I did find myself mesmerized by my own criticisms—*that idea doesn't belong there, that idea needs to be reworded, that idea needs to be better developed.* But being caught up in that state of mind would delay the creative process.

The most important thing at the outset is not creating a perfect sculpture. It is exploring new ideas in order to discover what you want to sculpt.

It's funny to say, but we must play. We must play around with ideas and be able to explore them freely. The purpose of this stage isn't to find the right idea, but to find many of them.

What happens next?

After all these trials and ordeals, after wandering around new intersecting streams of ideas in order to get closer to inspiration, it then becomes time for inspiration to find us.

Summary:

- 4th Stage: Trials and Tribulations of Finding New Ideas
- Archetype: The Wanderer
- Task: Explore and Play with Ideas
- Obstacle: The Siren of Censorship

The 5th Aspect
Retrieving the Reward

Entering the Darkened Cave

The doughnut maker took a quick glance at the sun. "So after you escaped the siren's song, were you able to control your exploration again and continue west?"

"I was able to get back in the right direction, but I wouldn't say I had much control."

"I can't imagine your travels getting any more difficult," replied the laborer. "Dangerous pits, dragons, vultures, sea creatures, pirates, sirens…"

"Do not be mistaken. The days immediately following my encounter with the siren would prove to be the most grueling."

The chef then inquired if there were even more creatures to battle.

"No." replied the beggar. "But as I tried to recapture my lost momentum, the weather turned on me. Winds came with heavy rain. There was little I could do but be led by the elements. My focus was on keeping myself afloat as the turbulent seas toyed with me. The clouds were thick and gray, so I saw no sun. But even if I did, I had no say as to my course. However, on the morning of the third day away from the siren, Mother Nature brought me to my destination, and I arrived at the island of the darkened cave."

"Was it a cave of dark pickle skin?" inquired the farmer.

"Or burnt doughnut shell?" inquired the doughnut maker.

"No. It was so named because there was only one small opening from above through which a ray of sunlight could enter into it. It was here the treasure lay hidden. It was a small cave, no larger than a doughnut hut. And because I arrived at sunrise, I imagined I had plenty of time to search for my reward."

The beggar noticed that the sun was now halfway through the horizon. And though the villagers were tiring, they displayed no signs of wanting to return to their homes.

"I began carefully inspecting the cave. I walked around and used my hands to feel along the cave's interior walls, hoping to find a hidden compartment or some removable object. Then, starting from the front of the cave, I began to dig through every inch of the cave floor until I hit hard dirt. Soon the sunlight began to dim. The day approached night faster than I had expected. I had looked for a chest or some sort of container, but found none. It then occurred to me that not only did I not know how to find the treasure, but I also was oblivious to what it looked like."

The villagers began to lie down on the grass. While their bodies were weakening, their minds were enthralled.

"Maybe, it wasn't the right season," the farmer commented.

"Maybe, you didn't work hard enough to find it," added the laborer.

"Maybe, you should have better planned your journey," remarked the religious person.

"All those thoughts crossed my mind," answered the beggar. "And as it grew darker, I became desperate. I began to yell and shout, calling for the treasure to appear, calling for help in my search…but nothing. I did this for hours after sundown to no avail. And before I realized it, I had fallen asleep with no idea of how I was going to change my predicament the next day."

Suddenly, a loud growl burst into the night air, startling the villagers.

"Relax," assured the beggar. "Don't let his snoring scare you. Your alcohol-induced friend has seemingly left us for pickle and doughnut dreams. Maybe, we should do the same."

"What?" a villager asked in distress.

"No! I need to know now what happened," added another.

"You can't just stop there!" exclaimed a third. "I want to hear how you dealt with this predicament."

The beggar leaned in towards the villagers. "Ok. I'll tell you."

The villagers remained silent, anxiously anticipating the beggar's next words.

"I slept on it."

The farmer looked at the laborer, who looked at the chef, who looked at the religious person, who looked at the doughnut maker, who looked at the village drunk, already soundly asleep.

"Slept on what, exactly?" asked the doughnut maker.

"There was nothing else I could do. So, I simply fell asleep. The next morning, the sunshine shot through the hole in the cave's ceiling striking me right between the eyes, and I awoke. But when I did, I had found it. I was given the knowledge of how to find the treasure. It had come to me in my sleep."

CHAPTER FOURTEEN
How to Attract Flashes of Insight

The one who keeps her heart awake,
Though the eye of her head may sleep
Her heart will open a hundred eyes.
– Rumi

The last aspect of the Creative Journey was pretty extensive, and I know there was a lot of material to digest. Not only are you now a creative hero entrusted with the Secrets of Out-of-the-Box Thinking, but you are also a creative apprentice, enthusiastically awaiting to further your training.

However, rather than just plowing on with reckless abandon, let's just take a moment and relax. Your brain has been working awfully hard lately, and it deserves a little break.

Take a few deep breaths, and try to simply sit here for a minute or two in silence, allowing your mind to simply float—unleashed and uncontrolled. And feel free to close your eyes, only if you feel comfortable doing so.

———◆———

Did you try to relax? If not, here's your second chance…

———◆———

If you actually did take a breather, did your mind wander, or was it still? Did any ideas come up for you while you were silent? Did you come in contact with any interesting thoughts, whether or not you feel they are useful?

If not, there is no need to fret. Just be aware that it is during these types of moments that insights often arise—moments when you least expect them. So keep your pen, paper, and voice recorder within reach at all times to capture that idea when it arrives.

The Story of Creative Insights

In the late 1940s, there was great effort made to help bridge two separate fields of physics: electrodynamics and quantum mechanics. To get a feel for this, just try to imagine how difficult it may have been a thousand years ago to bridge the notion of a falling apple with the rising and setting of the sun—both artifacts of the invisible force that we would later call gravity. They both seem related, but can be difficult to prove.

A young physicist named Freeman Dyson took the challenge head on. Both electrodynamics and quantum mechanics were descriptions of the physical world, but they each had their own separate branches of equations and laws. Like a good scientist, Dyson spent day after day for six months in Princeton reviewing stacks and stacks of calculations from both branches. But after the six months, he had wandered through these trials and ordeals for as long as he could. He simply could not come up with a bridge. So, he decided it was time for a change of scene, and he departed for a trip to California.

Hoping to quit his day job by striking gold perhaps?

No. Though he did not go to California to speak to other experts, to continue reviewing more documentation, or to continue working on equations. Instead, he did an even smarter thing.

For the next two weeks, Dyson did nothing but bum around.

He dropped his work completely.

At the end of his little two-week California getaway, he began his long bus ride home to Princeton without having made any progress on his quest. Then, one night during his bus ride, it hit him. He was struck by a sudden awareness. The way to bridge electrodynamics with quantum mechanics became apparent. "...that was sort of the big revelation for me, it was the Eureka experience or whatever you call it."

What we call it is a flash of creative insight.

Thinking by Not Thinking

Are you saying that in order to get a creative insight I have to bum around and do nothing?

It's not really about doing nothing. It's more about not doing what you think you should be doing—which is thinking about your creative endeavor.

Researcher Colin Martindale calls this "defocused attention." The theory is that the less intensely we activate our neural networks, the more neural networks can be activated. In other words, if we loosen our grip on our "idea" fishing net, a wider net can be cast out to sea.

- Thomas Edison was thought to explore new ideas by doing just that. In order to gain creative insight, he would try to sleep while holding heavy metal balls over metal pans. By doing this, he could enter a more defocused state but be awakened by metal clamor immediately before falling into unconscious states of mind.
- Many people have found insight through nighttime dreams when conscious awareness rests and the unconscious roams free. Writer Samuel Taylor Coleridge came out of a dream with the inspiration for his epic *Kubla Khan*. One day, he had fallen asleep while reading a work called *Purcha's Pilgrimage*. Three hours later, he awoke with ideas and images that inspired him to feverishly write the lines that would be the impetus for his epic.

There are numerous ways to reach these defused states. Just recall some of the circumstances where you found yourself with a creative insight. You may have found them while driving, while doing some fun reading, or while carrying on an unrelated conversation. You may have encountered insights during a walk, a jog or while gardening, folding laundry, or washing the dishes. Often they occur when in nature, but they can also occur when you wax your car, paint the fence, sand the floor, or browse a bookstore.

Many people simply sit, relax, and meditate.

Stress and Relaxation

Studies indicate that relaxation helps creativity in two fronts. One, there is evidence that it assists the creative process. Conversely, there is also evidence to think that stress may obstruct the process.

Relaxation and Creativity

In the previous chapter, I mentioned Nancy Andreasen's research that indicated a different brain activity when using free association—undirected thought which happens in a relaxed state of mind and is important for creative insight.

When we are in states of deep relaxation, such as before we fall asleep, the more specialized regions of our brain are less active. This level of activity corresponds to a slow measure of brain waves called *alpha waves*. It is in these alpha states—when our dominant neural networks aren't hot and bothered—that we tend to lose our focus, our ability to concentrate, and we start fantasizing about banana splits, flying reindeer, hot baths, and traveling gnomes.

At the same time, when our more specialized brain regions become less active, the brain as a whole gets highly active. Lessening the intensity of a few neural nets allows for a greater span of activity. To use a music analogy, toning down the volume of the brass section allows for more music to be heard from the rest of the orchestra. In this state, neurons are firing left and right. This level of activity corresponds to a fast measure of brains waves called *gamma waves*.

Like an orchestra that's warming up producing chaotic music, the gamma waves can be chaotic indicating a high-energy but chaotic symphony of the brain. However, these gamma waves can also appear in synchrony throughout the brain—like a high energy but *coherent* symphony—reflecting high level thought processes. Then, it's as if there is cooperation and communication between neural networks throughout the brain to integrate "complex information in order to discover its meaning or to solve a problem." [1]

As of the publication of Nancy Andreasen's book *The Creating Brain*, the highest levels of gamma synchrony had been measured in meditating monks. Using an objectless loving kindness meditation, the monks measured levels that corresponded to the number of hours they had spent practicing. Further, it was in the association cortices, the unspecialized regions, where the power of these gamma waves was the greatest.[2] Those unspecialized workers in our mental metropolis were flying all over the place, making frequent trips between the different parts of town.

In short, in states of deep relaxation, the specialized parts of the brain quiet down, while the unspecialized parts work to integrate all that it knows. It's then no wonder that flashes of insight occur when relaxing.

Stress and Creativity

First, it is under stress that our survival mechanisms are most active, which include our propensity for snap judgments and reactive responses. In order to be flexible enough to explore new ideas, we need to calm these down.

As I mentioned in Chapter 8, our emotions can have a direct influence on our thoughts, and our thoughts can perpetuate our emotional reactions. But that's not the whole story. Our emotions are dependent on a small part of the brain called the amygdala. But about only 5% of our sensory input enters it.[3] This means that our brain generates emotional reactions with very limited information.

By reacting to these emotions and associated thoughts, we can further perpetuate and exaggerate our emotional reactions that in turn keeps our perspective rather narrow—fight or flight, no negotiations. So in order to go beyond our initial emotionally charged thoughts and to allow more creative ideas to enter our awareness, it may be beneficial to relax, to allow our initial emotional reactions to calm down rather than perpetuate them.

A child who refuses to share her toy, the frenzied football fan in the stands, the terrorist filled with hate and fear, or the artist angry at her lack of productivity are all emotionally charged individuals having a hard time perceiving alternate views. By tempering our reactivity, not only can we gain access to a larger perspective, but we can also place ourselves in a position to better understand the nature of our charged feelings. This understanding may then help us to determine more appropriate responses to our circumstances, rather than automatically turning to our habitual ones.

Secondly, recall that learning new things requires the formation of new neural connections—the forging of new associations. One way of strengthening these connections, making them more ingrained in memory, is through repetition. To a limited extent, our hippocampus helps us do this when we are first exposed to something new.

Sometimes, when I'm trying to learn a new phone number, I just say it to myself over and over again at first, hoping that it sticks. This is especially true when I'm trying to remember the number of someone exceptionally cute. The hippocampus performs a similar function by maintaining reverberating loops through our neural nets when these connections are first formed.[4] For a short time at least, it does its best to keep new connections active.

However, when under stress, the body produces a wide assortment of chemicals including cortisol, a chemical that may lead to the degeneration of brain cells in the hippocampus.[5] In one experiment, rats were exposed to radiation that damaged their hippocampus. Afterward, they showed a lack of curiosity and no longer had the urge to explore their environment. Therefore, stress may damage the area of the brain critical for acquiring new knowledge and related to our craving of new experiences.

To recap, when we participate in any contemplative practice—whether it is sitting in silence, walking, meditating, praying, or any relaxation activity—we are benefiting from the reduction of stress and the tempering of emotional reactivity. In addition, these practices may help increase the level of synchrony and activity of the unspecialized regions of the brain, while also decreasing the activity of the more specialized ones. We are calming down our overactive neural networks and creating space to become aware of creative ideas generated by our unconscious. It's like quieting the inter-district traffic of our mental metropolis so that wide ranging communication between districts can be made more efficient.

We can enter this space in just about any circumstance. It doesn't have to be within a peaceful environment. As the jazz or comedic improviser will attest, we can enter this space while also being active on a stage. It's simply a matter of being attentive to the present moment, without worrying about what's to come or fretting about what has past. Like the baseball player whose total focus is solely on the next pitch, we can become more attuned to the present moment by focusing on the immediacy of experience. It isn't a matter of being surrounded by stillness. It's about having a certain type of stillness within us.

Are these flashes of insight from right hemisphere brain activity?

They may be. But let's be clear: the process of innovation or creativity requires both hemispheres, not just the right hemisphere. Too often books that speak of creativity make a hard right- vs. left-brain distinction. This itself is a rather left-brained way to look at it. By that, I mean it is an oversimplification that categorizes and makes a linear either/or distinction of something that isn't so clear-cut. In fact, categorization, labeling, and dualistic either/or thinking are often associated with left hemisphere activity. So it's rather hypocritical for *creativity gurus* to only look at the brain this way. Although I have given right hemisphere Ralph a lot of credit for our creative thinking, poor left hemisphere Lawrence deserves a good deal of credit too.

EEG studies indicate that creativity involves a great deal of communication between the two hemispheres. A look at split-brain patients reveals that they often exhibit normal behavior, but display little creativity. In these cases, both Ralph and Lawrence are healthy hemispheres, but because the connection between the two is severed, they are unable to talk to each other. Split-brain patients are unable to translate Ralph's creative ideas into the forms of expression that Lawrence provides.

In order to be creative, Lawrence and Ralph need to be on good speaking terms.

This could explain the *aha* experience that accompanies creative thinking because it is *after* Ralph's unconscious processing that we are made aware of new insights. Researcher Mark Jung-Beeman created an experiment were subjects were asked questions, such as "What is a single word that will produce compound words if combined with pin, crab, and sauce?" fMRI and EEG imaging indicated increased activity in the right hemisphere when the answer was attained through a "eureka-like" insight.[6] Once Ralph is able to do its processing, information is passed across to Lawrence and we become consciously aware of it. *Aha!*

Therefore, in order to be more creative, we need to exercise both hemispheres. It's just that Lawrence is naturally more exercised, so we must make a conscious effort to get Ralph off the couch.

CHAPTER FIFTEEN
The Stage of the Warrior

After passing through the stage of Trials and Ordeals, the creative hero has now become more conscious of her reality. She is able to see more alternatives, options, possibilities, or more depth of meaning in her life. After loosening the grips of the conscious mind in the previous stages, she is primed to uncover the breakthrough thoughts—the *aha* illuminations—that escaped the linear, sequential thinking of her left hemisphere.

The creative hero is now in a position to experience chance accidents as synchronicities that arise around her, primed to run into the luck of Pasteur. It is during the reward stage that she must turn things over to the right hemisphere, allowing the tortoise mind to incubate just as Amy Lowell did before receiving her poem *The Bronze Horses*.

These insights are well known to almost all artists, inventors, and anyone who has ever understood the punch line of a joke. Konrad Lorenz, the 1973 Nobel Prize winner for medicine, is also very familiar with the reward stage of the Creative Journey.

> This apparatus...which intuits...plays in a very mysterious manner, because it sort of keeps all known facts afloat, waiting for them to fall in place, like a jigsaw puzzle.... You must give a sort of mysterious pressure, and then rest, and suddenly BING, the solution comes.[1]

The flash of insight I received for my research while I was in a bookstore is a great example of this (see Preface). After having struggled to find any ideas on how to put together all my research on creativity, I stepped away from my "work" and decided to do what I most felt like doing. In this case, that was simply to wander around the bookstore and enjoy myself. It was only after I gave myself permission to "bum around" that I was struck by inspiration for how to organize my research.

Creative ideas always seemed to come when I least expected them. Oftentimes, they flooded into my awareness right before bed. Sometimes, they overwhelm me as if bursting through the doors of my awareness right as I wake up. They also occur in the most random places—walking around a store, while working out, or while listening to music in my car. This is why it can be helpful to carry some sort of idea pad or recording device wherever you go—though I don't recommend writing notes while driving.

I also spent a good amount of time at local coffee shops trying to find new ways of expressing the different neurological ideas found in this book—looking for a new metaphor, a new analogy, or just some way to lighten up the discussion. Sometimes, my brain would slowly bog down to a sputter, and I would give up, succumbing to my fatigue. But then, inspiration would strike, and I would throw a fit, upset that the ideas came only after I had shut down my laptop.

Of course, I had to accept that the ideas came *only because* I had shut down my laptop.

The Cave of Control

It is in this stage that we are to attain the reward of a creative idea, or ideas. The reward may be the inspiration for a poem, a novel, a painting, a song, an invention, or a solution to a problem. It may be a new way of making an old family recipe, a new way to invest funds, a new career path, or a new approach to dealing with community issues.

However, after walking across the Pit of Pessimism, defeating the Dragon of Dominant Ideas and Behaviors, and escaping the Siren of Censorship, the hero must enter her innermost cave to attain the reward. In the Creative Journey, this innermost cave is the Cave of Control, and it often holds the creative hero captive, appearing to the hero as a sanctuary, albeit a false one.

After allowing the imagination and creative spirit to roam free, we need space to allow our subconscious to incubate. Where it was important for the wanderer to *feel as if* they had time to wander, the warrior actually does need time to be patient, to listen to her tortoise mind, and to pay attention to clues or synchronicities that may illuminate the reward. But the Cave of Control is where we must face our most incessant desire, the desire to control this process. Mozart also knew that finding the reward in the innermost cave could not be accomplished through conscious will.

> When I am, as it were, completely myself, entirely alone, and of good cheer…it is on such occasions that my ideas flow best and most abundantly. Whence and how they come, I know not: *nor can I force them*…. What has been thus produced I do not easily forget, and this is perhaps the best gift I have my Divine Maker to thank for.[2]

The creative hero must resist the urge to want her creative ideas to arrive in a form of her preference or in the time frame she desires. She cannot dictate the manner in which the reward reveals itself but must let the reward show itself on its own terms, just as Claxton advocated when he wrote of befriending the tortoise mind. She cannot rationally wrestle her way through the incubation period. In fact, after having worked so hard in preparation for this stage, we must be a warrior and fight the urge to fight.

Why a warrior? Why not something more subdued?

You can use any metaphor or symbol that best reminds you of this stage and how to move past it. For me, the main task is to be courageous enough to have faith, trusting that the creative process will take care of itself. In my mind, the idea of a warrior best epitomizes this courage.

Childish Thinking

It is incredible to note what the data implies. As we've been discussing in the past few chapters, a lot of our creative activity occurs within the complex, unspecialized regions of the brain with very little pre-wired knowledge called the association cortices. Interestingly, these cortices are the most advanced and newly developed regions of the brain. Hence, it appears that our brains have evolved from more hard-wired faculties to structures that are more capable of creativity, more able to adapt to an ever-changing environment.[3]

The western world tends to value rational thinking over other modes of understanding, including inspiration. Yet our creative faculties are the newest and most biologically advanced aspects of our brain. This does not mean we throw reason out the window. It simply means that sitting around waiting for ideas and solutions from divine inspiration is not mere *childish* or *magical thinking*. It is actually a way to make use of the latest tool in our cognitive tool kit.

As we've seen in the past two aspects of the Creative Journey, it also means that being an adult isn't about leaving childish thinking behind. Being a truly mature individual means knowing how to incorporate childish thinking into our everyday lives.

Now we've gotten our innovative, creative, ingenious idea. So that's the end of the creative process, right?

We may have finally found a creative idea, but we haven't actually created anything yet.

Summary:

- 5th Stage: Retrieving the Reward
- Archetype: The Warrior
- Task: Fight the Urge to Fight
- Obstacle: The Cave of Control

The 6th Aspect
The Return Home

The Story's End:
The Curse of the Creative Journey

It was dawn. The sun's crown began to slowly break through the horizon, and the villagers rustled around the grass, trying to hide from its rays. The beggar had woken up much earlier. He sat up against the large oak tree wide eyed, watching the morning begin.

The land was now bare where the carnival had been just a few hours earlier. It had left without leaving a trace.

The remaining visitors slowly began to rise from their slumber. One by one the chef, the farmer, the laborer, the religious person, and doughnut maker all yawned and stretched.

The village drunk remained motionless on the ground.

"How did you sleep?" asked the beggar.

"Well," the villagers replied.

"Did you dream of pickles and doughnuts?" asked the beggar.

The villagers thought for a moment but couldn't recall their dreams.

"I do not remember my dream, but I do know what lingered in my mind after I awoke," replied the chef.

The beggar nodded as if understanding the chef's sentiments. Without missing a beat, he began his tale once again.

"I had walked across the bridge over the dangerous pit, set sail on a boat without any knowledge of how to use it, found myself face to face with a fire breathing dragon—an encounter that left me without a single pickle or doughnut—then had several battles with vultures, pirates, and sea creatures. Then I overcame the mesmerizing song of a siren and suffered through the wrath of Mother Nature as she finally led me to my reward."

The villager's faces lit up with excitement. Their sleepy eyes sharpened as they stared intently at the beggar.

"But you see, the journey isn't simply about finding the treasure. It is about bringing it back home with you. However, in order for me to do that, I had to travel back the exact same way I came."

"Oh no," the religious person said worriedly. "Does that mean you had to face the same challenges that blocked your path initially?"

"No…not face them. I had to embrace them. I had to transform them."

"Transform them?" asked the laborer.

The doughnut maker thought for a brief moment. "Do you mean like when transforming doughnuts with frying oil?"

"Do you mean like transforming baby pickle seeds into ripe pickle adults?" asked the farmer.

"In a way," replied the beggar. "You see, I had to initially surrender myself to the cave in order to find the treasure, but then, I had to use it as shelter to plan my trip back to the siren. I couldn't simply rely on another storm to take me back to her."

"Why would you return to the siren? Isn't she out of the direct path back to the island?"

"She is. However, I needed to transform her into a fairy, one that would help me pick and choose the battles that lay ahead. I needed her advice on when it was necessary to confront the dangers that stood in my way back and when it was best to avoid them. I knew my boat was in terrible shape, so I could not handle all the trials that I had dealt with earlier. And in fact, the boat did eventually fall to the sea stressed by the elements of the journey."

"Are you saying that you swam back to the island?"

The beggar chuckled at the thought. "I would have certainly died if it came to that. The boat sank just after I had transformed the dragon into an ally that could carry me back to the island's shore."

"That's incredible!" replied the laborer.

"Those deeds are not possible," added the farmer.

"You would have required magic to have done those things!" added the religious person.

"True. But you must understand, by retrieving my reward I was exposed to a curse. It was a curse that required me to find some way to befriend these past demons and have them assist me on my return home."

"And what would have happened if you had not done this?"

"If I failed, I was cursed with returning back to the island as a beggar."

The villagers stood stunned.

"But look at you," they said. "Look, you must have returned empty handed. You must have failed."

The beggar smiled and nodded in agreement. "It certainly looks that way."

"Then why should we partake of this journey if it leads to failure?" asked the chef.

With a piercing glare, the beggar replied, "Because no treasure can be found unless one attempts to find it. Remember why you are here, why you lingered after exiting the carnival. Remember why you are listening to a simple beggar. Are these not reasons enough to risk failure?"

———•———

CHAPTER SIXTEEN
Integrating the Two Worlds:
Manifesting Ideas into a Reality

The creative hero began her adventure by walking over the Pit of Pessimism into the ambiguous underworld. She then dispensed with the Dragon of Dominant Ideas and Behaviors and resisted the temptation from the Siren of Censorship. And now, after escaping the Cave of Control, she has finally emerged having formed new concepts and new perceptions.

Yet the creative hero is now faced with her greatest challenge: to take what she has learned from the underworld and integrate it into the ordinary world. Creativity coach Eric Maisel refers to this integration as the balance of the dream and reality realms.

> The very act of creating is a confrontation between dream and reality, a marriage of dream and reality.... Without a dream, the clay just sits there. Without the clay, the imagined jar holds no water. The dreamer rejects reality, the realist rejects the dream, the artist embraces both dream and reality. In your art and in your creative life, you uphold the dream and you respect reality. [1]

By integrating these two worlds, the Kellogg brothers were able to take the insight attained through their accident with grain and turn it into one of America's most popular cereals. In spite of accessing the creative spirit, Coleridge would not have been able to produce *Kubla Khan* if the creative underworld and ordinary world remained separated.

It is not enough to have the great idea; the great idea must come into fruition for it to be a creation. Otherwise, Gandhi would have simply *held a belief* concerning the powers of non-violence and would

194

not have also *actually led* a mass political movement.

A great deal of time has been spent in this book emphasizing the value of the unconscious mind, especially in the formulation of creative insights and ideas. And while it is important to surrender ourselves to the creative process, it is only by re-engaging it *consciously* that we can turn our creative insight into a creative behavior. The managing mind that was turned down during our time in the Cave of Control must be relied upon to help us manifest our creative ideas.

We can also think about this in term of the two brain hemispheres. It is in this final stage of the journey that a balance between the two hemispheres is critical. After Ralph has formed an association that sparked a moment of insight, Lawrence must now evaluate the insight, articulate it, and manifest it.

It is for this very reason that not all individuals with altered minds are able to create. Many lack the ability to reintegrate their unusual, novel associations of the underworld into something coherent and tangible to others in the ordinary world. It is through the balance of the totality of our being that we can manifest the divine breath in dance, artifact, and music that is both unique and meaningful.

Jamie Aebersold feels that this integration is so important to becoming a great jazz improviser that he highlights these ideas at the very beginning of his book *How To Play Jazz and Improvise*, one of the most widely used texts for beginning jazz musicians.

> The most successful musicians are those who can balance the left-brain knowledge with the creative right-brain. If you can play by ear (right brain), you'll find yourself limited to only what you know. If you over emphasize the left-brain, you may end up sounding like a well-oiled jazz machine but not too inspiring.... At all times be listening intently to what you are hearing in your mind...then try to analyze it and play it with the proper articulation and feeling. The object is to have both sides of the brain working together, in harmony with each other.[2]

By integrating these two worlds, the jazz musician has access to two types of entities. She has access to the learned fingerings, strokes, rhythmic patterns, pitch combinations, and other knowledge that she has spent hours developing and memorizing. At the same time, she also has access to the imagination needed to combine these things in interesting, unique ways.

From Obstacles to Allies

How are we supposed to bridge the ordinary world of our habits with the interesting ideas of the creative abyss?

For each aspect of the Creative Journey, there is a balance that needs to be struck. Every obstacle that the creative hero faced during the journey away from the island of her ordinary world must be transformed into an alley on her return home.

Siren of Censorship to Fluttering Filter Fairy

For instance, the creative hero must call upon the Siren of Censorship in a new form, as the Filter Fairy, fluttering by the hero's ear, providing words of discernment. The writer must become friends with their internal editor, allowing it to help her discern good writing from bad and good ideas from better ones. Italian author Grazia Livi was known to have spent a great deal of time filtering through the ideas in her writing logs, trying to determine which ones to develop and how.[3] Dance choreographer Twyla Tharp reminds us how we must learn to appreciate the Filter Fairy, as it is a significant part of the creative process.

> When I tape a three-hour improvisational session with a dancer and find only thirty seconds of useful material in the tape, I am earning straight A's in failure…. In many ways, the creative act is editing. You're editing out all the lame ideas that won't resonate with the public.[4]

This entails that the creative hero develop critical thinking skills. She must not just be an expert at coming up with wacky ideas, but must also learn the practical know-how that will be required for her to make necessary judgments.

Cave of Control to Oasis of Organization

The Cave of Control must also be integrated and transformed into the Oasis of Organization. While many creative artists are thought of as lacking in organizational skills, for some moment (even if only brief), they were able to organize their materials, their environment, their thoughts, and/or their time in a way that allowed them to express their creative spirit.

Without this organization, the musician, author, painter, or choreographer runs the risk of tinkering on her work forever or of lacking the materials to bring their work into tangible reality. The scientist must organize her equipment and plan experiments to test and verify her ingenious theory. Starbucks would only be an interesting idea if Howard Schultz did not have a plan to bring his vision to life. So too, a community advocacy group needs to organize a plan to implement a creative solution to a community problem.

The difficulty is in balancing organization with the patience needed to ponder—to plan without stunting the natural evolution of the creative process.

The Oasis of Organization is a fanciful way of saying you may need to plan, set schedules, give yourself deadlines, and organize your materials. The attributes that enable creative wizards to come up with the most novel ideas are the same attributes that keep us stuck in the abyss.

For instance, during the writing of this book, there were times when I allowed myself the freedom to write whatever I felt like writing. When inspiration grabbed me, I grabbed my laptop or took out my notepad and allowed inspiration to work through me without regard to structure, coherence, or grammar. But if I undertook my entire endeavor in this way, not only would it read like a nonsensical rambling of a mad man (not that it doesn't now), but I also would have never finished it. I would still be working on it without any end in sight.

In order to complete my creative endeavor, I had to set deadlines for myself, regardless of how arbitrary they were. I would ask people to read my work, though it was not complete, and then I would use their availability as my deadline dates for drafts. While trying to organize my manuscript and complete missing sections, I would set goals with rewards. *Once I finish this section, then I'll allow myself to listen to one track from a particular CD.* Or *no non-fat mocha lattes with extra whip until I complete the next section.*

The point is that we need to be able to switch modes of attitude and behavior during the creative process. We need to strike a balance between the incessant need to control the process and a lack of organization to complete it.

From Dragon of Dominant Ideas and Behaviors to Carriage of Communication

Balance is required also between our freedom to explore new ideas and our conforming to common modes of communicating. The creative hero needs to be able to take their creative inspirations and find some means of relaying them in a meaningful way to others.

In this sense, the Dragon of Dominant Ideas and Behaviors must be brought back to life as a Carriage of Communication. The familiar concepts and actions that the hero tried so desperately to run away from must now be called upon to communicate her novel concepts to the ordinary world. It is through the unique expression of familiar words, movements, sounds, sights, and materials that others can share in the experience of your creativity.

The Carriage of Communication transports the creative hero across the bridge between the two worlds by providing a means of communication that the ordinary world can relate to. The painter must rely on her painting technique, the chef on her cooking methods, the advertiser on her marketing expertise, and the author on her knowledge of the written language. Mozart would have had no masterpieces if he only heard music in his head but was unable to write them or play them for others. Similarly, solving a problem is rendered useless unless the creative hero has the means to communicate the solution to others or the ability to act upon it herself.

Riding the Carriage of Communication back into the ordinary world can be the most time consuming stage of the journey and often requires the most work. It was this stage that Edison was referring to with his famous quote, "Creativity consists of 1 percent inspiration and 99 percent perspiration."

Choices beyond Transformation

When I was soliciting feedback on my early version of this book, I found myself faced with two general groups of readers. On the one hand, there were people who felt uncreative—never thinking that the creativity they saw in others could possibly be a skill they could cultivate for themselves. For them, the discovery of new ideas was paramount. On the other hand, there were those who I referred to earlier as creative wizards, individuals who were experts at generating ideas but considered themselves novices at manifesting their ideas into a tangible reality.

I must admit that the majority of this book is spent speaking to the first group because, when thinking of "creativity," it is this group to whom literature on this topic most often speak. I am still a novice myself in many respects, and I hope to learn more about this entire process as time passes by. Still, to both general groups, I can impart one last piece of advice to help with the journey home.

You Need Not Be Alone.
When the journey home is what I seek
And the prospects of return are looking bleak
There is one thing alone that I have come to see
Alone, by myself, need not be.

Though I tussle, tug, scream, and fret,
My burdens I will not soon forget.
I struggle every moment not to place these on others.
I wish to face them alone, if I had my druthers.

However, no person is an island, a rock, a stone.
Though my journey is mine alone.
Time mustn't make me forget, sleep, or lose my soul.
We are all parts of a greater whole.

Since my arduous journey is of incredible length,
Seeking support is not weakness, but strength.
There is no shame in collaborative pursuits
More involved means more will bear fruits.

So when the journey home is what I seek
And the prospects of return are looking bleak
I recall the one thing alone that I have come to see
Alone, by myself, need not be.

Throughout my creative project of scribing this book, I have relied on many people to provide me aid. There were those who I conversed with, both with intent and in passing, who presented me the gift of great ideas. There were those who reviewed my work who provided a discerning eye when mine was dulled. My mentors were also there to provide encouragement and the structure to help me stay on track. And with my wonderful friends, I was able to have their collective skills and talents available to me throughout the process.

> Group creativity isn't meant just for groups. It is meant for any individual who wishes to make their journey a collaborative process, if only for particular points along the way.

Creative wizards, meet your local ordinary islander. Islander, give your local creative wizard a hug. A sea needn't separate you two. If Ralph never communicated with Lawrence, nobody would ever get a joke. So, why live with an exaggerated seriousness about your endeavor? If either one of these fellas are not up to par for your current task, why not seek a bridge to one outside of yourself? Are you resistant because you choose to be or because you do not feel as if you have a choice?

As you know, this book is all about accessing more choices.

The Magician

The archetype for the return is the Magician, for it takes magic to integrate opposites into a coherent whole. The Magician is an alchemist who takes the unique associations found in one world and transforms them into elements of another. Only through cunning wizardry and witchcraft can the creative hero transform her former obstacles into allies and tools. Professor Guy Claxton describes the magician elegantly as being a resourceful learner.

> The resourceful learner is able to attend to puzzling situations with precision and concentration, and also with relaxed diffusion.... She is able to analyze and scrutinize, but also to daydream and ruminate. She is able to ask questions and collaborate, but is also able to keep silent and contemplate. She is able to be both literal and metaphorical, articulate and visionary, scientific and poetic: to know as Madame Curie,

and to know as Emily Dickinson.[5]

As Claxton indicates, the Magician must be an expert at holding the balance between widening and focusing perceptions. The revolving door between the ordinary world and the underworld must always remain open and easily accessible. Whether it is the painter who needs to transform inspired imagery into fine lines and colors or the adult who takes a childhood passion and turns it into a livelihood, it is only by being conscious of both worlds that the creative hero can complete her journey.

Summary:

- 6th Stage: The Return Home
- Archetype: The Magician
- Task: Integration, Balance, Transformation
- Obstacle: Everything and Nothing—Janusian Thinking

PART III
Why: Traveling the Road Less Traveled

CHAPTER SEVENTEEN
Thinking Differently as a Creative Journey

By approaching the creative process as a journey, I have broken it down into stages hoping to make the creative undertaking less daunting. To begin with, you are often better off focusing on the very next step of your path rather than its end. Too often, we think ahead to our finished product, even though the next step is our immediate concern. In addition, we cannot design our future because there is so much that is out of our control. But, by being aware of the creative process, we can be mindful of how we approach it. We can design how we *think* of it.

The process is not necessarily a linear one. Speaking of it in linear terms simply makes it easier to describe with language. Throughout the process, you will most likely find yourself jumping back and forth between stages—from tinkering with new ideas to finding insights, back to tinkering, then to stages of judgments and organization, and back to tinkering again…. I think you catch my drift. It all depends on how extensive your creative endeavor is.

Also, you may experience occupying more than one stage at a time. As anyone who has ever written a quick letter or email knows, we can find ourselves in a constant battle between writing and editing. That's why it may be more accurate to think of these stages as different *aspects* of the creative process. The improvisational jazz musician needs to be in many stages at once while in the midst of playing a solo during a jam session. Though she must turn down the activity of her judgmental mind surrendering to the flow of creativity, the discernment mechanisms of her mind must be able to determine when she has gone astray and bring her back on track.

So, the jazz musician must simultaneously not only relax, work, and listen to the unconscious allowing ideas to come, but also be consciously aware enough to discriminate bad notes from good ones, adjusting accordingly on the fly. In essence, she is fighting the Dragon, escaping the Siren, exiting the Cave, and then integrating them all back again simultaneously—as if by magic.

If you really think about it, this is true of many—if not all—creative endeavors to some degree.

Know Thy Self: Creativity Practice and Training

Oftentimes, creativity workshops spend a great deal of time working on the "thinking outside the box" aspect of the creative process. When the average Joe and Jane think of exercising their creativity skills, they frequently imagine a brainstorming session or the exploration of wacky ideas. However, as we've now discovered, the creative process consists of several different phases. Thinking outside the box is only one aspect of the creative process.

It is important then to figure out the aspect of the creative process you may be deficient in and work on those particular skills. Maybe, you are naturally intuitive or insightful but have difficulty managing your time or organizing your thoughts. In that case, your creativity practice may include some practice in time management or in organizing your tasks. Similarly, if you are a free flowing explorer of ideas with a wild creative spirit, you may have difficulty focusing your energies on the specific steps needed to manifest your ideas. You may then want to practice focusing rather than free-associating.

The point is that becoming a better explorer of the creative process does not mean learning only how to let go and how to explore ideas. To strengthen your ability to be creative, you should address all the skills needed to manifest something unique in the world, including time management, rational thinking, setting goals, and planning. This also includes exercising the project specific skills needed in your creative endeavor, whether it is beefing up your writing skills, becoming a better musician, increasing your marketing knowledge, or enhancing your ability to read a financial statement.

This means you need to know yourself. You need to know who you are—what your tendencies and strengths are—so that you can practice those skills that you may lack.

The ironic thing is that by exercising your creative faculties, by being more creative, you actually learn more about who you really are. Remember, thinking of something new means transcending the bounds of conventional wisdom and groupthink. This is the only way to explore new ideas. Since creativity requires us to go beyond the limiting stories that we inherit from others, we also then become more in-touch with our authentic nature when we are creative. We step outside the confines of our habitual neural patterns in order to test out new connections between ideas. No longer bound by cultural norms means we can be truer to ourselves.

By participating in the Creative Journey, we also participate in a journey of self-discovery.[1]

Being Open to the Journey

The Creative Journey can take on many forms, and each hero will undoubtedly follow her own unique path. Though this book is here to provide a map of the landscape, your particular roads and turns will be unique. So in addition to being open to novel ideas, you also need to be open to the journey itself, allowing it to guide you along the appropriate path.

Being Open to Different Stages

Part of the key to completing the Creative Journey is accepting where we are in it. This is especially true if we are participating in projects where the stages are more pronounced (as opposed to improvisational activities). Sometimes, we are striving to make new associations, but our brains aren't in that mode. Instead they may be in the mode to be critical or in the mode to plan. When we get stuck, if by circumstance or physical state, and we are unable to use our time to do what we had planned, we are almost always in the perfect state to participate in another stage. We just have to realize it before our negative thoughts snowball into depression, anxiety, or frustration.

For instance, in writing this book, I often set goals about how I wanted to spend my writing day. I would plan to use certain hours of the day for writing new material and other hours for editing already written passages. The problem was that I frequently found myself without the inspiration to find new ideas when I wanted them and without the desire to edit when I had planned to edit.

By being open to the process, I was flexible enough to edit when I had planned to find new ideas or find new ideas when I had planned to edit. The journey is naturally an iterative process, so, to repeat, we need to be prepared to find ourselves jumping back and forth between stages and not be set in believing that we must be at any particular one.

The negative emotions that arise when things don't go as planned are simply feedback. Our task is to use our discernment to determine how the feedback should be interpreted. Does it mean we should be working on something else (if we should be approaching our endeavor from another stage), or is it simply process pains that we need to work through? It is difficult to give a generic, universal method of determining this. But my general guiding principle has been the following: *am I getting anywhere, or am I just treading water?* As long as I felt I was progressing, I felt at ease with my decisions.

Being Open to Your Specific Path

Partaking of the Creative Journey does not guarantee that you will complete it in the way you had envisioned it. You may enter the creative underworld—the sea of possibilities, discover some creative idea, and find that you are unable to manifest it successfully into a tangible reality. It does not mean your creative endeavor was a failure; it simply means your journey is not yet complete and that your path will be different than what you had expected.

Jeff Hawkins and Donna Dubinksy created a failed handheld device called Zoomer. It had the functionalities of a desktop computer, including the ability to print and send a fax. Unfortunately, consumers did not seem interested in a fax machine in the palm of their hands. To their credit, Hawkins and Dubinksy had reserved enough capital to survive the failure. We can articulate this by saying that, while they followed their creative spirit in creating Zoomer, they spent enough time in the Oasis of Organization to have prepared for the rough seas on their return home.

As a result, they turned their Zoomer failure into a much more successful device: the Palm Pilot.[2]

As another example, your creative solution to gang violence may not provide you with the results you had expected. However, through this "failure" you can evaluate, learn, and bring new knowledge to the table when you go through the process of determining an improved solution. Remember, scientists and innovators produced their most insightful work during the periods when they also produced their most mediocre work. The people at Zoomer would have never made the Palm Pilot if they never reached a failure point. They would have simply kept creating bad product that nobody would buy.

From the beginning of this book, I've noted that the one common attribute among all successful Creative Journeys is that the creative hero must maintain their motivation. Having a deep passion and love for the journey is crucial, for setbacks and failures will often occur. The creative hero must find the motivation to continue in the midst of darkness. They must have a strong desire to answer the call to be creative in order to maintain momentum to propel them through the creative process.

Making Creativity a Habit

By figuratively conceptualizing the different stages and elements of the creative process as a journey, I wish to honor the path by being aware of its uneven roads. It seems much easier to maintain the motivation to continue along a path if its hills and valleys are interpreted as fanciful stops along a grand adventure. It also seems to help make the creative process seem more fascinating, fun, and exciting. Most of all, by integrating various perspectives into my own unique vision, I hope to make the creative process more transparent in my life, allowing me to develop it as a habit.

As mentioned earlier, human beings use mental short cut rules of thumb for snap decisions that limit the possibilities of our behavior and limit the possible lines of inquiry we can pursue for problem solving or for generating unique ideas. These short cuts are often the barrier to our access to creative possibilities. However, short cut rules in general need not be the enemy of creativity. All of these techniques, strategies, or avenues through which we can explore new ideas can themselves be made into creative rules of thumb. They can become creative habits.

Imagine a series of possible outcomes or actions being represented by a search-tree, where each action is a branch that can lead to other possibilities. Our rules of thumb often direct our attention towards a certain path, while eliminating the necessity to explore others. These rules of thumb attempt to guide us down roads that appear more probable or fruitful.

Figure 19

While our rules of thumb make our decisions and behaviors simple and efficient, they often do not represent the best course of action. How many people do you know who have certain habitual responses to feeling incomplete? To feel more whole they may have a rule of thumb that has them buying a new book, or new clothes, or drinking a beer, or eating fast food, or yelling at a loved one. In terms of personal finances, maybe you know somebody that has a rule of thumb that presents only two options to deal with debt: either get a higher paying job or spend less.

In computer systems, creativity can be simulated through the use of a rule, one that transforms, suspends, or drops a lower one for the sake of exploring more options. Through this higher rule of thumb, new lines of inquiry can be opened up and new possibilities can be explored.

Figure 20

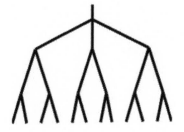

Similarly, we could do the same within our own minds. We could make creative thinking a higher rule of thumb. We can make thinking differently a habit or establish it as part of our normal routine. This could be in the form of setting some time daily, weekly, monthly, or yearly to reflect on our circumstances, beliefs, processes, and dominant behaviors and do the same type of exploration of ideas we have discussed throughout this book.

You could set aside some time every morning to free-associate. You could set aside a few minutes in every meeting to brainstorm. Or you could simply make it a habit to play devil's advocate, to daydream, or to *fiddle around*.

If our perceptions and behaviors are going to be frequently influenced by our mental short cuts, we might as well have a say on what some of those short cuts are.

CHAPTER EIGHTEEN
Trapped in the Abyss

One of the most dangerous aspects of the Creative Journey is that it can seem so appealing that we can become trapped in it. We can become so addicted to the prospect of the pot of gold at the end of the rainbow that we walk every false path hoping to find something that isn't there. The issue isn't in excessively participating in the Creative Journey per se but in thinking that it only involves the Sea of Possibilities and not the Ordinary World.

The process I have described in this book is not simply about finding new ideas, but also about finding something insightful that can be brought back to our shared islands, even if they are new insights arrived at from failure. However, we are sometimes unable to return from the creative underworld because we are either never able to reach the point of failure or are too lazy or arrogant to learn from them.

Addicted to Novelty

In this first case, I am specifically referring to when we become so in love with the romance of creative ideas that we completely ignore the return home. We love the pursuit of novelty, but have no interest in the hard work, the discernment, the organization, or the skills needed to bring our ideas to life. In Chapter 6, I refer to the daydreamer who constantly fantasizes about how the grass is always greener on the other side. This person loves to buy books but never reads them or loves to buy paint supplies but never paints.

Novelty addiction also includes those times when we love to only tinker and scratch but are frustrated when we haven't found success. We may fiddle around on the piano but are unwilling to practice, learn, or are simply unwilling to put in the sweat needed to work through a composition. We may think we have all the answers but are unwilling or unable to participate in implementing them. We may start projects without the needed dedication or willingness to work hard enough to complete them.

Tinkering and scratching is fine in their own right, but we can't expect to complete the creative process while only participating in this aspect of the journey. It is great to be an idea person, but then we need the wherewithal to surround ourselves with others who can help manifest our ideas into reality. Exploration can be fun, but we cannot neglect the necessary transformation of the Siren into Filter Fairy, of control into organization, or of the dragon into a carriage that is required for your return home. Otherwise, we'll be stuck, lost, wandering aimlessly at sea. And if we never even attempt the return home, we'll never have a chance to learn from failure.

Addicted to Our Assumptions about the Path

If we are privileged enough to fail, our greatest error would be not learning from it. This can occur when we are arrogant of the assumptions we place on our creative path. We can become so convinced that our failures have nothing to do with our approach to the creative process that we end up repeating the same mistakes. We are so sure that our assumptions about the process are correct that we continually ram our boat into a large rock because we are convinced that our path goes through there. We are oblivious to the fact that our approach is fundamentally flawed: *It's not me; it's them!*

One example is the restaurateurs who are so enthralled with their idea of a good restaurant that they completely ignore feedback they receive from customers up until their business collapses. Another is the day trader who always claims his/her system is on the brink of massive returns but continues to make losing trades. They are so attached to their creative idea that they close themselves off to any wisdom naturally available to them throughout the process. By being open to this wisdom, the people at Zoomer were able to chart a new path to success.

Another example of this is when we continuously jump to the next miracle diet without learning about the fundamentals of nutrition and weight loss or when we constantly chase after the next get rich quick scheme and pass it off as entrepreneurship. In this case, our assumptions are based on some sort of naiveté or arrogance in thinking we can partake of an easy path through the Creative Journey.

This reminds me of the joke where a man is on the top of a hill waiting for God to rescue him from a great flood. A boat comes to rescue him, but he rejects it saying he has faith that God will come and save him. A second boat comes by, but he rejects it too saying he has faith that God will come and save him. A third arrives only to be rejected on the same grounds. Eventually, the flood gets the best of the man, and he dies and goes to heaven. Upon arriving, he asks God why He didn't save him. And God replies, "Who do you think sent the three boats?"

We simply can't put expectations like that on the creative process. It needs to lead us more than our directing it. The more we force the path to be a certain way, the harder it will be for us to hear, see, or feel where it wants to take us. If we are so focused on the promise of the latest diet plan, we may neglect to see the flashing neon sign of the gym located across the street from our house.

The Illusion of Creativity

When we are addicted to novelty or addicted to assumptions on our path, we may feel as if we are being creative, but we have really just fallen prey to another rule of thumb. While addicted to novelty, we may be operating off of a rule of thumb that says *fulfillment can only come from external satisfaction*, so we become addicted to the abyss and the creative ideas that can be found there as if it were a drug. When we are blindly attached to our dominant notions of the creative path, we may find ourselves habitually implementing a number of heuristics, including some sense of *I have to be right* or one that says that the *creative path should be easy*. In both cases we lack the openness to accept that our perception of the creative path is flawed, regardless of the feedback we receive from the external world.

So in many ways, when we are apparently trapped in the abyss, we may have really never left our island. Our pursuit of a reward is only an illusion when, in fact, we haven't even crossed the pit or found the boat. We may believe we are thinking differently but are, in fact, simply habitually attracted to the idea of novelty or addicted to our ingrained assumptions of what the path should be.

Accepting the Journey for What It Is

We must remind ourselves to accept the reality of the Creative Journey—that there are times when we will hate what we are doing or what we have done. To be an explorer on this path, we have to push on just the same. To quote myself, "Sometimes, this journey really sucks... but the rewards are worth the trip."

The journey will contain difficulties that must be accepted before they are transcended. This is why I feel it is so important to have a guide for the creative process. We can all fall prey to any number of obstacles that stand in our way. When we encounter them, we can either be overwhelmed by them or be oblivious to their presence.

Without an understanding of the creative process, we may find ourselves stuck in some stage of the journey without any notion of how to move forward or without any idea why we are stuck in the first place. In order to overcome being trapped in the abyss, we need to be aware that such traps exist. By having some comprehension of what to expect, we can become more aware of the obstacles that block our path and have a better understanding of how to overcome them.

As a wise television program once pronounced, "knowing is half the battle."

CHAPTER NINETEEN
Answering the Call to Think Differently

There are as many reasons why somebody should participate in the Creative Journey as there are reasons to do anything else in life. Some of us want to get rich, have great sex on demand, or simply want to save the world. As I have hopefully shown, we need not strive to be the next Dickinson, Dali, Galileo, or Gandhi to follow the Creative Journey. However, no future Dali or Gandhi will exist if the path is not followed.

As I mentioned at the beginning, thinking differently is how we open up our awareness to what is possible. Like a blind rat in a maze, we often only shift directions when we run into a wall. Even then, we sometimes simply try to run through them and end up with a headache. For this reason, thinking differently can be thought of as a way of increasing the degrees of freedom in our lives.

Instead of living like a handicapped rodent, why not live like a creative artist. We can all be artists of how we live our lives. We can always choose to dance a new dance or to add a splash of color to our existence.

The Creative Journey provides a path to a wider range of solutions to a problem or ideas for improvement. Hence, all aspects of life can benefit from the Creative Journey, both personal and global. But as a result of my research, in addition to its benefit as a problem solving, freedom expanding, and idea discovering process, I have found other contexts through which others have framed its significance.

Creativity as Social Force

The Creative Journey has been brought into the spotlight lately and in ways I had never thought of. Richard Florida, Professor of Regional Economic Development at Carnegie Mellon, has written a whole book on how creativity is the driving force of social and economic change. Through his book *The Rise of the Creative Class*, he looks at how it is not technology or knowledge that is the driving force of the market place. Instead, he sees a new social class as being the driver.

Previously, the marketplace drove employees to locations with high-end jobs. Now many corporations are moving to areas with the highest density of quality employees. According to Florida's research, his ranking of high-tech hotspots seemed to correlate with areas that had large concentrations of artists, writers, and performers. Also, they seem to be areas of great diversity, including areas with large gay populations.[1]

Florida concluded that "rather than being driven exclusively by companies, economic growth was occurring in places that were tolerant, diverse, and open to creativity because these were places where creative people of *all* types wanted to live."[2] In addition, because companies desired creative employees, the workplace has evolved within the past fifty years to be conducive to this creativity. As a result, both society and the economy are now greatly influenced by a new class of individuals that he has termed the *creative class*.

Creativity author Ernie Zelinski notes that higher educational institutions are now adapting to this creative class.

> The most successful people in the new millennium will be highly creative people who are flexible thinkers and can deal with rapid change…. Educational institutions are seeing a need to teach creativity. Creativity is showing up in…graduate programs at universities. For example, several business departments at American universities, such as the Graduate School of Business at Stanford University, have courses in enhancing personal creativity…. It is the special talent that develops the right market segment. It is the ability that turns a crisis into an opportunity.[3]

Though higher education may be beginning to address the need for more employees with creative skills, there may still be a need to adjust the basic philosophy of an education system that stresses memorization of facts, rather than an exploration of meaning.

Educator Peter Kline writes in his book *Why America's Children Can't Think* that our educational system is stifling our children. He points to how more than ever, especially in an Internet age, our children will have to be proficient readers. However, standardized testing produces a population that can follow instructions but kills the creative minds of our children. He stresses that "no child should ever be asked to read a sentence that doesn't lead to a discussion and speculation about its personal meaning."[4] His emphasis seems to be that students may learn to read and understand literally but are not taught to think about what they have read, to be able to find deeper meaning, value, or creative comprehension.

Einstein explicitly said that imagination was more important than knowledge.[5] Unfortunately, the prevalent western paradigm seems to place more value on the critical faculties of mind simply because they are easier to test and measure.

Yet creativity isn't just for the student. In many classrooms, it often seems that teachers are forced into being simply a mediator of information. They become performers trying to get across certain ideas and lessons in order to meet some standardized educational goals. However, each student is different and classrooms are dynamic entities.

In order to best help our students think creatively, the teacher must also then have the freedom to engage them in an organic way.[6] Teachers must be allowed some freedom to creatively improvise following their students' interests in the material and allowing classroom discussions to stray off course in order to help students pursue personal meaning in the material at hand.

The only way to help students think for themselves is to give teachers the leeway to allow for creative exploration of ideas that deviate from the intended plans of the day.

Creativity for Healing

Beyond reading comprehension and beyond joining the creative class, the ability to plunge into the depths of meaning allows us access to multiple contexts in which we see others and ourselves. This includes the ability to see others *as* ourselves—overcoming a major obstacle in healing relationships between people and cultures.

As I have tried to illustrate throughout this book, much of our emotional anguish is the result of our misuse and overuse of certain habitual patterned responses to our environment. Some of us have a tendency to want to control everything or a tendency to continually grasp for satisfaction in our external world.

We also have emotional habits. We may walk into a room of strangers and feel anxious, scared of what they may be thinking about us. We may have a constant desire to please others. Such habits have their roots in our upbringing and may have been a very critical and necessary coping mechanism for our younger selves. Though, because we are often unaware of our habits, we may continue to use them to our detriment.

Being creative also means exercising the faculties of mind that help us realize these patterns and help us see that there are other ways of being in the world.

The ability to change the context in which we see our lives also allows us to frame our distress, pains, and illnesses in ways that make them more meaningful and manageable. Books like *Creative Healing* by Michael Samuels, M.D., and Mary Rockwood Lane, R.N., M.S.N, delve into how creative arts can help the ill recognize suppressed feelings or recontextualize their ailments in ways that not only make them have a better sense of well-being and hope, but also help spur on the recovery process.

Many times our pains are compounded by the story we tell of them. Just as we can perpetuate our emotions with our thoughts, we can also perpetuate or give strength to our pains by virtue of our addiction to our stories. Clinics around the country are beginning to acknowledge this and have developed pain management techniques to help patients alter their perception of their ailed states. By changing the stories we tell ourselves of our ailments—whether they be stories of self-blame, victimhood, fear, hate, hopelessness, or anger, we may be able to reduce our experience of pain.

Our mental dispositions also go beyond a tempering of psychological suffering. Evidence is beginning to show just how strongly our attitudes, understanding, and mental disposition can affect our physical well being. Within indigenous cultures, shamans use song, dance, and story to bring a deeper meaning to the ailments of the ill. This seems to promote the body's natural healing mechanisms, triggering its inherent defense systems.[7]   An entire field of research called psychoneuroimmunology is dedicated to studying the affects the mind can play in our body's well being. The research is particularly interested in the placebo affect, the idea that just the *thought* of receiving a cure could somehow cause the body to respond as if it actually did receive it. In such cases, the meaning we attribute to something—the context in which we experience the world—appears to have physical, material consequences.

Creativity as Honoring the Sacred

From a spiritual perspective, one reason—if not *the* reason—to participate in the Creative Journey is because it is a sacred act. Rather than be creative for all the rewards that can be gained, one is to be creative for the divine. In her book *The Artist's Way,* Julia Cameron frames the entire artistic endeavor as participating in a communion with God.

> When we open ourselves to exploring our creativity, we open ourselves to God: Good Orderly Direction…. Creativity is God's gift to us. Using our creativity is our gift back to God.[8]

This leads us to another reason for answering the call of the creative hero. That is, we should participate in the creative process because it is our intrinsic nature to be creative. All things change, and survival depends on the ability to adapt. Hence, nature is inherently creative, and so too are human beings. We neglect this nature for all the reasons the hero has difficulty traveling her creative path—fear, lack of optimism and hope in something better, complacency in the habits of dominant ideas and behaviors, judgments, and an unwillingness to be patient with the creative process.

Yet, we know that our brains have evolved to be able to see different perspectives, create new ideas, and attain creative insights. So, not only is creativity part of our being from a spiritual perspective, but also from a biological one. And to me, regardless of one's spiritual leanings, being true to oneself—even on a purely philosophical basis—can be a sacred act.

Answering the Call for Happiness

The reality is that nobody can tell somebody else why they should be creative. According to research performed by Teresa Amabile, the most successful creative hero does not answer the call for reward or material gain but simply because they love what they are attempting to create. In fact, the prospect of external expectations and reward can actually be a detriment to the journey because they may curb intrinsic motivation.[9]

Playing music, painting, sculpting, dancing, writing, and thinking divergently, all may play significant roles in manifesting a strong society, bridging cultural boundaries, keeping one healthy, and in deepening access to possibilities. But the main reason why the musician sings, the painter paints, the dancer dances, and the writer writes is because they enjoy doing it.

All we can do for others is encourage them and place value on their journey. We can give reasons why it should be taught and promoted in business, education, communities, and families. But in order to be most successful, we should answer the call not because we have to, but because we want to—because it makes us happy.

CHAPTER TWENTY
Life, Liberty, and the Pursuit of Meaning

The neuroscientific picture of human cognition illustrates the intricacies and nuances of our perception, our problem solving, and our decision-making processes. Though we usually go about our day unaware of the depths and complexities involved in our mental activity, they always exist beneath our habitual reactions to life's coarse terrain.

In light of what I have learned about our cognitive faculties, I feel there are implications for how we view our less literal-minded pursuits. These are methods that our ancestors had used for ages to make sense of the world but are often now viewed as having little significance because they seem to lack practical application. Yet, after our tour of the creative process, we can see how they are not only practical, but necessary for exercising the meaning deepening traits that are critical to our creativity.

By utilizing the power of thinking differently, we may help heal the wounded soul.

Art, Games, and a Sense of Play

Creativity seems to be the mind's most recent evolutionary skill. Yet creativity is often treated as a subservient talent, one that needs to take a back seat to the cultivation of our rational faculties. In order to best use our natural evolutionary advantage, our educational curriculum, and society as a whole, needs to encourage activities that foster and exercise our ability to build new conceptual associations.

As adults, the world can seem full of important responsibilities and critical actions. However, when was the last time any of us faced the threat of immediate attack from a lion, bear, or other predator?

Our actions are critical but we are hardly ever in a life-threatening situation that requires us to keep our snap judgments in peak working condition. More than fight or flight, the challenges that we face today require thinking differently, and to cultivate this, we need a cultural shift toward valuing games and a sense of play.

Every once in a while, we can shed our serious demeanor and indulge in activities for fun rather than for 'practical takeaways.' Sports and the arts are great examples of such pursuits. Our consideration here is not the activity's impact on our income, career, lifestyle, or status in society, so we can stop worrying about being *correct* and simply have fun enjoying the activity for its own sake.

When we were children this came easily since our instinct was to first learn as much as we could about our environment—and our place in it—rather than being cautious and correct. However, over time, our defense mechanisms took over emphasizing the need to be cautious and right in order to avoid emotional or physical harm. This made us serious, "practical" people. We start seeing our favorite games of make-believe as flights of fantasy. We start believing that our interest in theater, music, dance, visual arts, creative writing, board games, puzzles (and a whole assortment of activities) is purely recreational and therefore not 'practical.' Now we know better. These very activities exercise our creative thinking muscles allowing us to strengthen our latest evolutionary skill.

Through these activities, we can cultivate a creative environment for groups, and we may learn to bring back the attitude of exploration, lightheartedness, and play that were once our natural attributes as creative children. Though they often seem like long lost friends, these attributes still reside in each of us. You would not have picked up this book if that were not true. All they need from us is a little cultivation for them to blossom so that they may return to affect our daily lives.

Maintaining a Peaceful Heart

Science asserts that a deeper grasp of reality can be gained through the formation of new associations that occur when we have space to relax, where we can weaken our pre-existing dominant neural connections. So too, many of the world's great traditions emphasize methods for living one's life that weaken dominant thought patterns.

- Taoism's principle of *wu-wei* encourages a person to live with simplicity and without resistance to the underlying currents of the universe—the Tao. In essence, it is the practice of going with the flow of life, rather than struggle to exert control over every aspect of our existence.
- Buddhism emphasizes the need to be aware of our thoughts and to be mindful of our actions to avoid getting caught up in our habitual thoughts and desires. Remember Bert and Ernie? Simply speaking, it is by being mindful that we can better handle the habitual thought patterns that are the roots of so much mental anguish.
- Hindu yogas often emphasize letting go of the desires of our finite self by identifying with the infinite. One way to relate to this is by realizing that the story we tell ourselves of who we are is always limited. By realizing this, we can free ourselves of the pain and frustration associated with defending these stories or maintaining them for the sake of others.
- The same release of dominant thought patterns are attained by exercising the western notions of forgiveness, faith, and surrender. All of these notions are ways of coming into acceptance of our present circumstances, letting go of the need to control what we cannot control.

These are only a few of many personal practices that encourage us to live life in a non-survival mode. They dim the intensity of the stress mechanisms that activate our snap judgment faculties, providing us with the conceptual space and cognitive flexibility to be more receptive to creative ideas and insights.

While the creative process is naturally arduous, it can be made less so by journeying with a peaceful heart.

Science of the Whole Mind and Its Implications for a More Complete World View

Reason has proven to be an excellent tool for releasing human beings from the grips of dogma and superstition. However, there has been an undesirable side effect to the rightful condemning of harmful behavior (witch burning, human sacrifices, gender inequality, racial inequality etc). The western world has come to devalue many frameworks of meaning for their apparent lack of rational grounding. In particular, the rich mythology and religious contexts that our ancestors once used to frame their lives are now often viewed as unsophisticated and intellectually inferior compared to scientific paradigms.

From within the framework of cognitive science, the meaning of any concept is based upon the associations it has with other concepts. When we think of duct tape, a web of associations is triggered: the color silver, the concept of tape, its circular packaging, household repair, miscellaneous past experiences we have had with it, and many others things. Because these associations determine its meaning, the larger the web, the more meaning-*full* duct tape will become. This deepens our understanding of what it is and what it can be used for.

At one time, the dominant perception of duct tape was *tape used to seal ammunition cases*. Thinking differently has allowed the dominant perception to change and become *tape used for luggage, musical instruments, furniture, automobiles, cookware, spacecraft, noisy children, and numerous other applications*. To think of it differently—creatively—is to search for alternative associations to our dominant perception, thereby constellating a deeper, more comprehensive understanding.

While the deepening of our understanding of duct tape has proven extremely useful, it underscores how much more depth of meaning is possible for our perceptions of our own lives and of our relationship to the world we live in. Whereas new applications were made possible for duct tape, this deepening can help us realize new ways of living in a turbulent world. Seeing beyond the immediate, literal, dominant, filtered, limited understanding that our own internal neural structures help formulate, we can achieve a more accurate impression of what it means to be human. For a culture whose common sense is based on a literal materialism, forming a deeper context may require the use of less literal lenses.

This is where myth and religion come in. Unlike the hard sciences, mythology and religion open up multiple perspectives and access to associations otherwise not possible, through their use of symbolism, metaphor, and analogy.

The wide array of stories, poems, dance, songs, and other elements of a tradition help us to constellate a deeper view of who we are below the surface of our 'persona.' Even a peek into reality through its most popular elements can be deepening.

- By looking at our daily suffering through the lens of Moses' travels through the desert, we may be able to see them as elements of a rewarding path rather than meaningless struggles.
- Some of us can get caught up in the tangents of life, sidetracked from pursuing our heart's desire. By seeing life through the framework of Homer's *Odyssey*, perhaps we can be more cognizant of temptations in appealing guises and other pitfalls that await us on life's journey.
- There are major concerns over the condition of the planet and the depletion of natural resources. The personal relationships between man and nature that are so prevalent in myths of indigenous people may help humanity develop a more beneficial relationship to the earth.

We all possess, or are possessed by, meaning making paradigms. We all have underlying narratives that we use to make sense of ourselves, the world, and our place in it. The question is whether or not we are aware of them and whether or not the ones we do have are of our own choosing or are simply the default paradigms of culture.

It's the pursuit of value that deepens our understanding of our selves and our world, not the pursuit of literal fact. The meaning of the duct tape deepened when its usefulness widened. Physically, the duct tape remained a duct tape. Our pursuit of literal meanings and our pursuit of value have different purposes and are attained through different methods.

To allow mythologies and religions to help us, we need to be consciously aware of them—of when and why we view ourselves and the world through their lenses. If they become another rule of thumb, we end up with terrorism or persecution. It would be as if we loved music so much that we attempt to use it to calculate the maximum weight an elevator could hold. "That's absurd!" you may exclaim. But that's what we do all the time. We love jamming round pegs into square holes because we can become so enamored with round pegs.

Only conscious awareness of our stories or pegs will help us choose appropriate ones—old or new, round or square.

Our culture holds critical thinking way above creative thinking, while we now know these are important processes that need to be implemented in cooperation. Creativity is an important skill needed to generate new ideas or new stories and to discover new paths to follow. Critical thinking is a skill needed to test the validity and usefulness of these ideas and to help illuminate the road along new paths.

For a more complete or meaning-*full* worldview, left hemisphere Lawrence and right hemisphere Ralph need to be active. Lawrence is really active in individuals with an abundance of knowledge through experience, i.e., wisdom. Conversely, Ralph busts his tail for those who think creatively.

Then, to be both wise and wily, one would expect to have to use their entire brain.[1]

Re-enchanting the World

By choosing to live in a literal world run by our initial, dominant perceptions of experience, life can seem void of alternatives, choices, possibilities, and new perspectives. But the consequences of this go far deeper than the inability to create a new invention, paint a new painting, remedy social issues, or begin a new business venture. By living a life trapped in our familiar perceptions, we lose our appreciation for the special-ness and uniqueness of every moment. We become so accustomed to its colors and sounds that we no longer appreciate, or notice, its inherent variety. As a result, life can become dis-enchanting, devoid of novelty, mystery, and soul fulfilling meaning.

Does the word *enchanting* conjure up images of folklore and fairy tales, the stories that filled our lives with magic and wonder when we were children? Most of us lose this sense of awe and mystery as we grow older. However, this sense of mystery is the spark that ignites our creative passions and leaves room in our lives for creative possibilities. This sense of mystery allows us to experience life more fully, in all its radiance, its inherent uniqueness, mystery, and ambiguity. Things aren't always the way they seem. There is always more to the story of our experience.

For instance, a wooden chair need not simply be a wooden chair (the dominant, literal meaning). The story that we use to assign it meaning does not have to end there. The chair could also be used as firewood. It could be used as a doorstop. The chair may be used whole, or in parts, as a weapon for self-defense. The chair also has its own history. There may have been some noteworthy events in your past that involve it, including usage at a rowdy bachelor or bachelorette party. It also had a history before arriving in your possession. This includes where it was sold, how it was manufactured, and all the parties involved from its birth to it's being situated in your home. And because of this, each chair is unique.

You can see that the chair need not just be a chair. It can be special. In fact, it is special. There is not one other chair like it anywhere in the world. The same is true of every house we drive past, every tree we walk by, and every person we meet. They all have their unique stories that make them multidimensional, more special than we initially perceive them to be, and they may help illuminate new associations relevant to our own lives. It's only our habitual pattern recognition that blinds us to this fact.

In a similar vein, as you also saw with the example of the duct tape, we can always expand meaning in our lives by reframing our experience of the world. We can frame our lives in terms of a movie, book, song, story, game, fairytale, joke, riddle, or any other context that provides us with a more empowering perspective. This is what I have tried to do by reframing the creative process into a heroic journey. Seemingly, the breadth of meaning accessible to us is only limited by our imagination. The more we are able to perceive our lives within multiple frameworks, the more we are able to see possibilities, opportunities, hope, reasons for compassion, reasons for forgiveness, and reasons for cheer.

We have also all experienced the enchantment of life on a more visceral level. Think back on all those special moments, if only brief, that inspired and moved you. There may have been moments under the moonlight, a starry sky, or while staring out at sea that engulfed your attention and placed you in a state of wonder and awe. There may have been a moment on your first date or a reunion of lost friends or family that made life seem more than ordinary. There may have also been moments when you were struck by the inner beauty exuded by the kindness of strangers or the sheer terror of the darkness and the destructive potential that reside in others.

The world never is just this way or that way. Neither is it always out to get us, nor is it just full of red roses and happy accidents. The world is always more. Adults often dismiss the authenticity of fairytales because they can seem fanciful and utopian. Yet this is a skewed perspective of the enchanted world. We neglect the horrendous fact that Little Red Riding Hood's grandmother was eaten alive by a wild beast—a cross dressing one at that! We trivialize the notion that Sleeping Beauty was in a coma, that Cinderella was a slave to her stepmother and stepsisters, and that Hansel and Gretel were abandoned by their parents—left for dead in the darkened woods.

What we remember is that many of these tales end well—the characters living happily ever after. This does not fit within our literal framework, and so, we feel as if they are irrelevant to the real world. Within a creative framework though, they are just the right resource for our journey. Remember the first two tasks in the creative process:

1.   Believe that alternatives may be possible.
2.   Have hope that they are worth pursuing.

What better example of this than the enchanted world of a fairy tale? This is what makes them relevant to our adult lives.

Every once in a while, it pays to look at the world through a soft focus lens so that we can experience the inherent depth of meaning that exists everywhere. By doing so, we not only free ourselves of habitual, literal perceptions, but we also allow space for creative insight to manifest, where we can experience the special-ness of the moment.

Utilizing the power of thinking differently means finding a balance between living in a literal world and an enchanting one fraught with creative possibilities.

If we were to ignore the practicality of living, we would find ourselves trapped in the abyss. If we ignored the depth of meaning available to us through our creative faculties, we would be stuck in the ordinary world, unable to experience anything more than the monotone world we have conditioned ourselves to experience.

Weddings, birthdays, holidays, anniversaries... all these cultural traditions are, at their roots, meaning-enhancing events, but too often, we participate blindly out of obligation or habit and we don't experience the true depth of meaning there. It isn't that the world is special only on certain occasions or in certain moments. The world is always special. It is simply that we are often very preoccupied with our ingrained perceptions, very numb to our experiences of the world to notice.

The wonderful thing about understanding the science of thinking differently is that you now have an acceptable rational lens through which you can begin to appreciate the inherent enchantment of the world. Understanding that the world is necessarily more than your experience of it means the world is naturally more meaningful, wondrous, and unique than you can ever know. Through the power of thinking differently, you can see the sunset, the seasons, your job, your home, and your loved ones from a fresh perspective making them even more enchanting. Every moment can be novel because there is an infinite number of ways to experience it. Through the power of thinking differently, the mystery and ambiguity that existed for us as children can return to supplement the pragmatic perceptions we hold as adults; just as the creative hero must reside in both the ordinary world and the creative underworld.

It is common to search far and wide for precious moments, meaningful lives, and intimacy with awe; these are simply different aspects of the motivational spark that drives us to explore new ideas, solutions, and perspectives. They are the motivations that drove Benjamin Franklin to explore the nature of electricity and drove Shakespeare to write plays that explored the nature of man. Therefore, whether we are fully aware of it or not, the desire for enchantment underlies many of our motivations. So while talk of re-enchanting the world may seem fanciful in some respect, it is simply a way to express that behind everything we encounter lies a mystery waiting to reveal creative possibilities.

Practicality of Thinking Differently: Creativity in Everyday Life

We usually associate creativity or thinking differently with special projects—pieces of art, discoveries, inventions, business endeavors, corporate productivity. When you need to solve a problem or design a new product you may think of creativity or out of box thinking. In the meanwhile, we continue with our pattern recognition mechanisms in our everyday lives, experiencing and responding to situations on autopilot. In many ways, several of the difficulties we face today can be attributed to an unbalanced use of our intellectual tool kit. We apply pattern recognition to our everyday scenarios—like with the carrot, the pipe, and the button in the field—only to discover that our solutions don't work.

What is needed is to counterbalance our snap decision mechanisms with creative thinking. Thinking differently and the creative insight it often provides are critical for the continued evolution of humanity, especially in light of the growing complexity of her environment. In order to fully take advantage of this evolutionary gift, we need to become aware of all the aspects of our lives that we may be operating on automatic—our finances, our professional career, our personal relationships etc—and occasionally take time to reevaluate.

So why not participate in the creative endeavor? Why not think of yourself as a creative hero partaking in an adventurous journey of transformation: from innocent, to orphan, to martyr, to wanderer, to warrior, to magician, and back again? Why not leave the comforts of your island to explore turbulent seas and face dragons, seductive sirens, and dark caves in order to find and bring home your reward: your unique, ingenious, innovative, inspired, creative ideas and perspectives?

You may claim that you lack the free time to live and behave creatively, but the habitual short cuts that we employ often waste more time by leading us down wrong paths or by making us trod along them inefficiently.

Even more importantly, utilizing the power of thinking differently is the only way we can claim to be living our own lives rather than somebody else's. It is only by approaching our lives creatively—making our decisions through conscious awareness of possibilities rather than through habitual responses—that we can honestly ever say we are truly living it.

And this, in my mind, is truly a heroic undertaking.

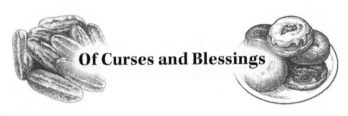

Of Curses and Blessings

The villagers continued to sit on the grass with the beggar by the old oak tree. They were contemplating.

When the sun had risen the day before, they had entered the yearly carnival. It was a reprieve from the winter's storm that left their village in turmoil. And later, after exiting it, they were enthused by what they had experienced there. They had found hope for living differently.

By chance, they had wandered toward the tree, finding each other and a beggar with a tale to tell of his exploits off the island. It was a tale of an arduous adventure—a journey that consisted of difficulties, unrest, but one that promised a reward that could change their lives on the island. It was a reward that could help them improve a village left in less than ideal circumstances by the recent winter storms. It was also a reward that could help them be better prepared to deal with an ever-changing world.

Now, after finishing his tale, the beggar simply sat and waited. He waited for a response from the villagers who had so eagerly listened to the accounts of his travels.

"I'm hungry," said the laborer.

"Me too," added the farmer.

The chef grabbed his sack full of food that he had taken with him into the carnival. He had been so preoccupied with the day's events that he had neglected to take even one bite from what he had brought.

"Well?" interrupted the beggar. "Do you accept the challenge?"

The villagers looked at the ground as if hoping to find direction there. Then, they all looked at the food placed in their hands by the chef, and they looked at each other's food. They looked at each other's shriveled pickles and doughnuts.

"But how can we?" asked the doughnut maker. "You said the boat was wrecked at sea."

"Fear not. A new boat always awaits those beginning a new journey."

A new journey, they thought to themselves. The words caused their spines to tingle and their palms to sweat. *Do we dare explore and find ourselves in the midst of a world more than just pickle soup, pickle huts, doughnut drums, doughnutty government, and doughnutty economies?*

They thought back on their routines and their inability to find new ideas on how to change their lives. And then they looked at the beggar and thought *being exploring beggars seems better than being stationary village people.*

"I accept the challenge, beggar!" exclaimed the chef.

"So, do I!" added the religious person.

The chef, the religious person, the doughnut maker, the farmer, and the laborer all jumped onto their feet.

"We will take your experiences, beggar, and depart in search of our reward," said the farmer.

"And we will return to redeem you of your failed endeavor," added the laborer.

"Failed endeavor?" questioned the beggar. "I didn't say I failed. I only said that it looks that way."

"What?" replied the doughnut maker. "Then, you have brought the treasure back with you?"

"Of course," the beggar quickly answered.

"Then why haven't you shared it with us?" demanded the laborer.

The beggar stood up from underneath the tree and calmly replied, "What do you think I have been doing?"

Smiles came across the villagers' faces.

"Now go. Take my treasure so that you can find your own."

And with those final words, all the villagers left to travel west towards the other side of the island.

Well…almost all.

The drunk was left behind, as he continued to stay soundly asleep.

Once they reached the other side of the island, they crossed over the dangerous pit and found a brand new boat waiting for them at the shore. Meanwhile, back by the old oak tree, just as the villagers set sail, the beggar's clothes were magically transformed into fine linens and the beggar's appearance sharpened. It was only now that he had finally completed his journey, and so the curse was lifted. It was only now that he was transformed into something completely different—his authentic form. And with his newly found treasure, he too was ready to begin exploring once again.

———◆———

www.Thinking-Differently.com

Notes

Introduction
[1](Wakefield, 1996, p 6-7)

Chapter 1
[1](Rothenberg, 1990, p 8)

Chapter 2
[1]This section draws heavily on *The Medici Effect* by Frans Johansson
[2](Johansson, 2004, p 80)
[3](Johansson, 2004, p 79)
[4](Zelinski, 1998, p xxi)
[5](Perkins, 2000, p 28)
[6](Johansson, 2004, p 75)
[7](Csikszentmihalyi, 1996, p 110)
[8](Sandblom, 1992, p 47)
[9](Wakefield, 1996, p 88)
[10](Andreasen, 2005, p 81)
[11](Wakefield, 1996, p 51)
[12](Wakefield, 1996, p 9)
[13](Cameron, 2002, p 1)
[14](Crockett, 2000, p 2)

Chapter 4
[1](Piattelli-Palmarini, 1994, p 37)
[2](de Bono, 1991, p 5)
[3](Piattelli-Palmarini, 1994, p 52)
[4]The probability of a tail being flipped is ½. The probability of a head being flipped is also ½. The probability of any independent consecutive sequence of flips is equal to the product of their probabilities. In this case, since the two possible outcomes of a coin flip have equal probability, every sequence of a particular number of flips will also have equal probability. For example, for two consecutive flips of a coin HH, HT, TT, TH the probabilities are each $(1/2)*(1/2)$, or ¼. Likewise, every possible sequence of seven flips has a probability of 1/27, or 1/128.
[5]Again, the probability of any independent consecutive rolls of the die is equal to the product of their probabilities. A sequence of RGRRR has the probability of $(2/3)*(1/3)*(2/3)*(2/3)*(2/3)$, or 16/243. A sequence of GRGRRR has a probability of $(1/3)*(2/3)*(1/3)*(2/3)*(2/3)*(2/3)$, or 16/729. And, a sequence of GRRRRR has a probability of $(1/3)*(2/3)*(2/3)*(2/3)*(2/3)*(2/3)$, or 32/729.
[6](de Bono, 1973, p 32)

Chapter 7
[1](Goleman, 1992, p 20)
[2](Zelinski, 1998, p 23)

Chapter 8
[1](Ornstein, 1986, p 36)
[2](Wexler, 2006, p 96)
[3](Wexler, 2006, p 156)
[4](Wexler, 2006, p 157)

Chapter 9
[1](Restak, 2003, p 158)
[2](Restak, 2003, p 10)
[3](Ornstein, 1997, p 103)
[4](Ornstein, 1997, p 108)
[5](Ornstein, 1997, p 70)
[6](Goldberg, 2005, p 202)
[7](Goldberg, 2005, p 203)
[8](Restak, 2003, p 25)
[9](Goldberg, 2005, p 214)

Chapter 10
[1](Johansson, 2004, p 81)
[2](Greene, 1999, p 112-116)

Chapter 11
[1](Andreasen, 2005, p 77-78)
[2](Wakefield, 1996, p 8)
[3](Bianchi, 2006)
[4](Vera and Crossnan, 2005)
[5](Williams, 2002)
[6](Hargadon and Bechky, 2006)
[7](Amabile & Khaire, 2008)
[8](Hargadon and Bechky, 2006)

Chapter 12
[1](Ornstein, 1997, p 73)

Chapter 13
[1](Tharp, 2003, p 94)
[2](Johansson, 2004, p 96)
[3](Johansson, 2004, p 112-113)

Chapter 14
[1](Andreasen, 2005, p 163)
[2](Andreasen, 2005, p 164)
[3](Bennett-Goleman, 2001, p 108-109)
[4](Goldberg, 2005, 112-114)
[5](Dispenza, 2007, p 282)
[6](Goldberg, 2005, p 205)

Chapter 15
[1](Claxton, 1997, p 58)
[2](Claxton, 1997, p 94) (Ghiselin, 1985, p 34-35)
[3](Goldberg, 2005, p 104-105)

Chapter 16
[1](Maisel, 2005, p 176-177)
[2](Aebersold, 1997, p 2)
[3](Csikszentmihalyi, 1996, p 80)
[4](Tharp, 2003, p 213)
[5](Claxton, 1997, p 221)

Chapter 17
[1]The reader may be interested in reading Homer 2006, Maslow 1962, or Runco 1999.
[2](Johnson, 2004, p 132)

Chapter 19
[1](Florida, 2002, p 235-266)
[2](Florida, 2002, p x)
[3](Zelinski, 1998, p xiv)
[4](Kline, 2002, p 24)
[5](Zelinski, 1998, p 2)
[6](Sawyer, 2004)
[7](Tedlock, 2005, p 14-20)
[8](Cameron, 2002, p 3)
[9](Amabile, 2001) (Johansson, 2004, p 138)

Chapter 20
[1](Goldberg, 2005, p 218)

Bibliography

Adams, J. (1986). *The care and feeding of ideas: A guide to encouraging creativity.* Reading, MA: Addison-Wesley.

Aebersold, J. (1992). *How to play jazz and improvise.* New Alabany, IN: Amey Aebersold Jazz, Inc.

Amabile, T., & Khaire, M. (2008). Creativity and the role of the leader. *Harvard Business Review,* 86, 100.

Amabile, T. (2001). Passion craft of creativity. *American Psychologist,* 56, 333-336.

Andreasen, N. (2005). *The creating brain: The neuroscience of genius.* New York: Dana Press.

Anonymous. (2008). National Institute on Deafness: In jazz improv, large portion of brain's prefrontal region 'takes 5' to let creativity flow. *NewsRx Health & Science,* March 10, 51.

Balachandra, L., Barrett, F., Bellman, H., Fisher, C., & Susskind, L. (2005). *Improvisation and Mediation: Balancing Acts,* 21, 425-434.

Barron, F. (1963). *Creativity and psychological health.* New York: D. Van Nostrand Co.

Bianchi, A. (2006). In the mood for creativity. *Stanford Social Innovation Review,* 4, 9.

Bennett-Goleman, T. (2001). *Emotional alchemy: How the mind can heal the heart.* New York: Harmony Books.

Beth, H., & Amabile, T. (1998). Reality, intrinsic motivation, and creativity. *American Psychologist,* 53, 674-675.

Binnewies, C., Ohly, S., & Sonnentag, S. (2007). Taking personal initiative and communicating about ideas: What is important for the creative process and for idea creativity? *European Journal of Work and Organizational Psychology,* 16, 432-455.

Boden, M. (1991). *The creative mind: myths & mechanisms.* New York: Basic Books.

Bono, E. (1984). *Future positive.* New York: Penguin.

Bono, E. (1991). *I am right, you are wrong: From rock logic to the water logic.* New York: Viking.

Bono, E.D. (1973). *Lateral thinking: Creativity step by step.* New York: Harper Paperbacks.

Bono, E. (1968). *New think: The use of lateral thinking in the generation of new ideas.* New York: Basic Books.

Bragdon, A. G. (2000). *Building left-brain power: Conditioning exercises and tips to strengthen language, math and uniquely human skills.* New York: Barnes and Noble Books.

Breen, B. (2004). The 6 myths of creativity. *Fast Company, 89,* 75.

Cameron, J. (2002). *The artist's way: A spiritual path to higher creativity.* New York: J.P. Tarcher.

Cassou, M. (2001). *Point zero: Creativity without limits.* New York: J.P. Tarcher.

Claxton, G. (1997). *Hare brain tortoise mind: How intelligence increases when you think less.* New Jersey: The Echo Press.

Csikszentmihalyi, M. (1996). *Creativity: Flow and the psychology of discovery and invention.* New York: HarperCollins.

Damasio, A. (2003). *Looking for Spinoz: Joy, sorrow, and the feeling brain.* Orlando: Harcourt Press.

Dietrich, A. (2004). The cognitive neuroscience of creativity. *Psychonomic Bulletin & Review,* 11, 1011-1026.

DiGiacomo, A. (2007). "The creative envelope": A theoretical model of the creative process in music therapy through psychodynamic and humanistic perspectives. *The American Journal of Psychiatry,* 165, 1615-1616.

Dispenza, J. (2007). *Evolve your brain: The science of changing your mind.* Deerfield, FL: HCI.

Florida, R. (2002). *The rise of the creative class: And how it's transforming work, leisure, community and everyday life.* New York: Basic Books.

Franzini, L. (2002). *Kids who laugh.* Garden City Park, NY: Square One Publishers.

Fritz, R. (1989). *The path of least resistance.* New York: Ballantine Books.

Gelb, M. (2002). *Discover your genius: How to think like history's ten most revolutionary minds.* New York: Harper Colins.

Ghiselin, B. (1985). *The creative process: A symposium.* Berkeley: University of California Press.

Glynn, I. (1999). *An anatomy of thought.* New York: Oxford Press.

Goldberg, E. (2005). *The wisdom paradox*. New York: Penguin Group Inc.

Goleman, D., Kaufman, P., & Ray, M. (1992). *The creative spirit*. New York: Dutton.

Goleman, D., Kaufman, P., & Ray, M. (1992). The art of creativity. *Psychology Today*, 25, 40.

Greene, B. (1999). *The elegant universe: Superstrings, hidden dimensions, and the quest for the ultimate theory*. New York: W.W. Norton.

Greenfield, S. (2000). *Private life of the brain: Emotions, consciousness, and the secret of the self*. New York: John Wiley & Sons.

Gregory, B. (1988). *Inventing reality: Physics as language*. New York: J. Wiley.

Hargadon, A., & Bechky, B. (2006). When collections of creatives become creative collectives: A field study of problem solving at work. *Organization Science*, 17, 484-500, 525.

Horner, A. (2006). The unconscious and the creative process. *Journal of the American Academy of Psychoanalysis and Dynamic Psychiatry*, 34, 461-469.

Howard, P. (1999). *The owner's manual for the brain*. Austin, TX: Bard Press.

Jalan, A., & Kleiner, B.H. (1995). New developments in developing creativity. *Journal of Managerial Psychology*, 10, 20.

Johansson, F. (2004). *The Medici effect: Breakthrough insights at the intersection of ideas, concepts, and cultures*. Boston: Harvard Business School Press.

Johar, G., Holbrook, M., & Stern, B. (2001). The role of myth in creative advertising design: Theory, process and outcome. *Journal of Advertising*, 30, 1-25.

Johnson-Laird, P. (2002). How jazz musicians improvise. *Music Perception*, 19, 415-442.

Kline, P. (2002). *Why American's children can't think: Creating independent minds for the 21st century*. Makawao, Maui: Inner Ocean.

Kutschke, B. (1999). Improvisation: An always-accessible instrument of innovation. *Perspectives of New Music*, 37, 147.

Martindale, C. (1981). *Cognition and consciousness*. Homewood, IL: Dorsey.

Maslow, A. H. (1962). *Toward a psychology of being*. Princeton, NJ: D. Van Nostrand Co.

May, R. (1975). *The courage to create*. New York: W. W. Norton & Company.

Minsky, M. (1988). *The society of mind*. New York: Simon & Schuster.

Nachmanovitch, S. (1990). *Free play: Improvisation in life and art*. Los Angeles: J.P. Tarcher.

Ornstein, R. (1986). *Psychology of consciousness*. New York: Penguin Books.

Ornstein, R. (1997). *The right mind*. New York: Harcourt Brace & Company.

Perkins, D. (2003). *Archimedes' bathtub: The art and logic of breakthrough thinking*. New York: W.W. Norton & Company Inc.

Pearson, C. (1986). *The hero within: Six archetypes we live by*. San Francisco: Harper & Row.

Phillips, H. (2005). Looking for inspiration. *New Scientist, 188*, 40.

Piattelli-Palmarini, M. (1994). *Inevitable illusions: How mistakes of reason rule our minds*. New York: Wiley.

Platt, R. (2003). *Eureka!: Great inventions and how they happened*. Boston: Kingfisher Publications.

Provine, R. (2000). *Laughter: A scientific investigation*. New York: Viking.

Ramachandran, V. B. (1998). *Phantoms in the Brain: Probing the mysteries of the human mind*. New York: William Morrow.

Rao, C. (2005). Myth and the creative process: A view of creativity in the light of three Indian myths. *Creativity Research Journal, 17*, 221-240.

Restak, R. (1994). *The modular brain: How new discoveries in neuroscience are answering age-old questions about memory, free will, consciousness, and personal identity*. New York: Scribner's.

Restak, R. (2003). *The new brain: How the modern age is rewiring your mind*. Emmaus, PA: Rodale.

Rothenberg, A. (1990). *Creativity and madness: New findings and old stereotypes*. Baltimore: John Hopkins University.

Runco, M. A. (1999). Self-actualization. *Encyclopedia of Creativity, 2*, 533-536.

Samuels, M., & Lane, R. (1998). *Creative healing: How to heal yourself by tapping your hidden creativity*. San Francisco: HarperSan Francisco.

Sandblom, P. (1992). *Creativity and disease: How illness affects literature, art and music.* New York: Marion Boyars.

Sawyer, K. (2000). Improvisation and the creative process: Dewey, Collingwood, and the aesthetics of spontaneity. *Journal of Aesthetics & Art Criticism,* 58, 149

Sawyer, K. (2004). Creative teaching: Collaborative discussion as disciplined improvisation. *Educational Researcher,* 33, 12-20.

Shaddock, D. (2006). My terrible muse: Cohesion and fragmentation in the creative self. *Psychoanalytic Inquiry,* 26, 421-441.

Spitzer, M. (1999). *The mind within the net.* Cambridge, MA: The MIT Press.

Stevens, A. (1991). *On Jung.* London: Penguin.

Stevens, T. (1995). Creativity killers. *Industry Week,* 244, 63.

Sternberg, R. (1998). *Handbook of creativity.* Cambridge: Cambridge University Press.

Tedlock, B. (2005). *The woman in the shaman's body: Reclaiming the feminine in religion and medicine.* New York: Bantam Books.

Tharp, T. (2003). *The creative habit. Learn it and use it for life.* New York: Simon & Schuster.

Vera, D., & Crossnan, M. (2005). Improvisation and innovative performance in teams. *Organization Science,* 16, 203-224.

Vogler, C. (2007). *The writer's journey: Mythic structure for writers.* Studio City: Michael Wiese Productions.

Wakefield, D. (1996). *Creating from the spirit. A path to creative power in art and life.* New York: Ballantine Books.

Ward-Steinman, P. (2008). Vocal improvisation and creative thinking by Australian and American university jazz singers: A factor analytic study. *Journal of Research in Music Education,* 56, 5-17.

Wexler, B. (2006). *Brain and culture: Neurobiology, ideology, and social change.* Cambridge, MA: The MIT Press.

Williams, S. (2002). Self-esteem and the self-censorship of creative ideas. *Personnel Review,* 31, 495-503.

Zelinski, E. (1998). *The joy of thinking big: Becoming a genius in no time flat.* Berkeley: Ten Speed Press.

Index

Index (continued)

Index (continued)

Index (continued)

Index (continued)

Acknowledgments

My Creative Journey in writing this book has been long and arduous. It was an adventure that I could not have completed on my own, and I owe a great deal to the many guides and companions that have helped me along the way.

Several individuals provided feedback on the many versions of this manuscript. I am very grateful for all of their comments and suggestions—especially those that challenged my own perspective. In particular, I owe many thanks to my very own Filter Fairy, my editor Liza Joseph. The return to the ordinary world would have been impossible without her. I felt safe exploring my own creative abyss knowing that everything I wrote would pass through her critical eye.

Furthermore, the manifestation of my ideas into a tangible book was in no small part due to the hard work of my book designer Susan Reed. I also am very grateful to my cover designer, and good friend, Christine Nolasco. I was very lucky to have Christine's creative genius work on the brilliant exterior design of this book.

When I first took a hiatus from my engineering career, I never dreamed that it would lead me to publishing a book on creativity. Many thanks goes to Marilyn Fowler and Peter M. Rojcewicz, PhD at JFK University for giving me the freedom to pursue my wild independent research projects into "thinking differently" and to all my instructors who provided me with guidance, encouragement, and inspiration throughout my Creative Journey. I could not have asked for a better environment to pursue my research. I am also forever indebted to the many students at the University whose ideas and perspectives helped me constellate my own.

Throughout the years, several other individuals have influenced my creative life. Thanks goes to every music director I have ever worked for, every music instructor I have had the pleasure of working with, and to every single student that I have had the privilege of teaching—especially those of you that went to school near a rodeo (you know who you are). Moreover, I owe a great deal to all my writing, English, and communications teachers who encouraged my weirdness and found value in my eccentric prose.

During the process of putting together *The Power of Thinking Differently*, I was faced with various differing critiques from readers and confronted with many difficult decisions. When I needed a trusted opinion to help me make final choices and a sounding board for ideas, I turned to one of the most creative people I know—Matt Harvey. His insights and honest feedback were invaluable in the formulation of the final version of this book. He also just may be the fastest reader in the galaxy, or within a 10-mile radius of my house at least. It was an honor to have him involved in this project. Even more, it is an honor to be able to call him my friend.

Finally, I owe all that I am to my favorite fraternity: *Mamma, Papa, Sister*. For over three decades, my family has provided me with the space to think differently. Words cannot justly express the profound influence they have had on my life, not to mention this book. However, what I can say is that it was through them that I learned to appreciate the value of a sense of humor.

Yes. You can blame them for it.

About the Author

Javy Wong Galindo, M. Eng., is a self-proclaimed creative dimwit who is working very hard to become better. This former electrical engineer and performing arts teacher has over 13 years of experience providing creative consultation. He is also co-owner of a company devoted to spreading the healing power of humor.

When he's not speaking on creativity, Javy can be found singing at a club, performing bad comedy improv, writing an unfunny comedy sketch, running poorly on an uphill trail, or attempting to catch flies with chopsticks.

AVAILABLE FOR PUBLIC SPEAKING & CONSULTATION

Workshops – Seminars – Lectures – Coaching – Training – Encouragement

LEARN MORE ABOUT
The Power of Thinking Differently

Visit: www.thinking-differently.com

49877218R00155

Made in the USA
San Bernardino, CA
07 June 2017